Special Thanks

to

Fresno Unified Science Specialists

Care Butler
Evalyn Hoover
Sharon Kinnear
Howard Larimer
Sheryl Mercier
Betsy Olson
Hal Silvani
Jeri Starkweather
Peter Summers
Mike Walsh

The writers also wish to thank
the many classroom teachers in Fresno Unified
who willingly shared many creative ideas.

Primarily Physics

INVESTIGATIONS IN SOUND, LIGHT, AND HEAT FOR K-3

Editors

Judith Hillen

Sheryl Mercier

Evalyn Hoover

Betty Cordel

Principle Authors

Evalyn Hoover

Sheryl Mercier

Contributing Authors

Howard Larimer

Karen Adler

Mike Walsh

Illustrators

Sheryl Mercier

Margo Pocock

Consultant

Dr. G. Bradley Huff

Science Coordinator

Fresno County Office of Education

Fresno, CA

This book contains materials developed by the AIMS Education Foundation. **AIMS** (**A**ctivities **I**ntegrating **M**athematics and **S**cience) began in 1981 with a grant from the National Science Foundation. The non-profit AIMS Education Foundation publishes hands-on instructional materials (books and the monthly *AIMS* Magazine) that integrate curricular disciplines such as mathematics, science, language arts, and social studies. The Foundation sponsors a national program of professional development through which educators may gain both an understanding of the AIMS philosophy and expertise in teaching by integrated, hands-on methods.

ISBN 1-881431-46-0

Printed in the United States of America

I HEAR, AND I FORGET
I SEE, AND I REMEMBER
I DO, AND I UNDERSTAND

–Chinese Proverb

Project 2061 Benchmarks

AIMS is committed to remaining at the cutting edge of providing integrated math/science studies that are user friendly, educationally sound, developmentally appropriate, and aligned with the recommendations from national education documents.

Below you will find a listing of the *Benchmarks for Science Literacy* (American Association for the Advancement of Science) which are addressed in this publication.

- *People can often learn about things around them by just observing those things carefully, but sometimes they can learn more by doing something to the things and noting what happens.*

- *Things change in some ways and stay the same in some ways.*

- *When a science investigation is done the way it was done before, we expect to get a very similar result.*

- *Science investigations generally work the same way in different places.*

- *Tools such as thermometers, magnifiers, rulers, or balances often give more information about things than can be obtained by just observing things without their help.*

- *Describing things as accurately as possible is important in science because it enables people to compare their observations with those of others.*

- *When people give different descriptions of the same thing, it is usually a good idea to make some fresh observations instead of just arguing about who is right.*

- *Everybody can do science and invent things and ideas.*

- *In doing science, it is often helpful to work with a team and to share findings with others. All team members should reach their own individual conclusions, however, about what the findings mean.*

- *Numbers and shapes can be used to tell about things.*

- *Tools are used to do things better or more easily and to do some things that could not otherwise be done at all. In technology, tools are used to observe, measure, and make things.*

- *When trying to build something or to get something to work better, it usually helps to follow directions if there are any or to ask someone who has done it before for suggestions.*

- *Change is something that happens to many things.*

- *The sun warms the land, air, and water.*

- *Things that make sound vibrate.*

- *Magnifiers help people see things they could not see without them.*

- *People use their senses to find out about their surroundings and themselves. Different senses give different information. Sometimes a person can get different information about the same thing by moving closer to it or further away from it.*

- *People can learn from each other by telling and listening, showing and watching, and imitating what others do.*

- *Numbers can be used to count things, place them in order, or name them.*

- *Simple graphs can help to tell about observations.*

<u>***Students should:***</u>

- *Raise questions about the world around them and be willing to seek answers to some of them by making careful observations and trying things out.*

- *Describe and compare things in terms of number, shape, texture, size, weight, color, and motion.*

- *Draw pictures that correctly portray at least some features of the thing being described.*

Processes

	Observing	Predicting	Classifying	Comparing/contrasting	Communicating	Collecting/recording data	Interpreting data	Drawing conclusions
Sound is Vibration	X	X		X	X	X	X	X
Traveling Sounds	X	X		X	X			X
Paper Cup Telephone	X			X	X			X
Musical Bottles Xylophone	X	X		X	X	X		X
Sound of Voices	X	X		X	X			
Eggs-Full of Sound	X	X			X	X		X
Big Ears	X	X			X			X
Which Way?	X	X			X	X	X	X
The Eyes	X				X	X		X
Light Sources	X		X	X	X			
Mirrors Reflect	X	X			X	X	X	X
Just Passing Through	X	X	X	X	X	X		X
Light Rays Slow Down	X			X	X	X		X
I ♥ Color	X	X		X	X	X	I X	
Magnify	X			X	X			
Prism Power	X	X		X	X			X
What is Hot and What is Cold?	X		X		X	X		
Heat Energy From Friction	X			X	X			
Hot or Cold?	X	X		X	X		X	X
What is the Temperature?	X			X	X	X	X	
Melt an Ice Cube	X	X			X	X	X	X
Heat Energy and Color	X			X	X	X	X	X
When Hot and Cold Meet	X	X			X			X
Heat Energy Moves	X	X			X	X	X	X
Heat Energy Travels	X				X			X
Cold Tin and Hot Hands	X				X	X		X

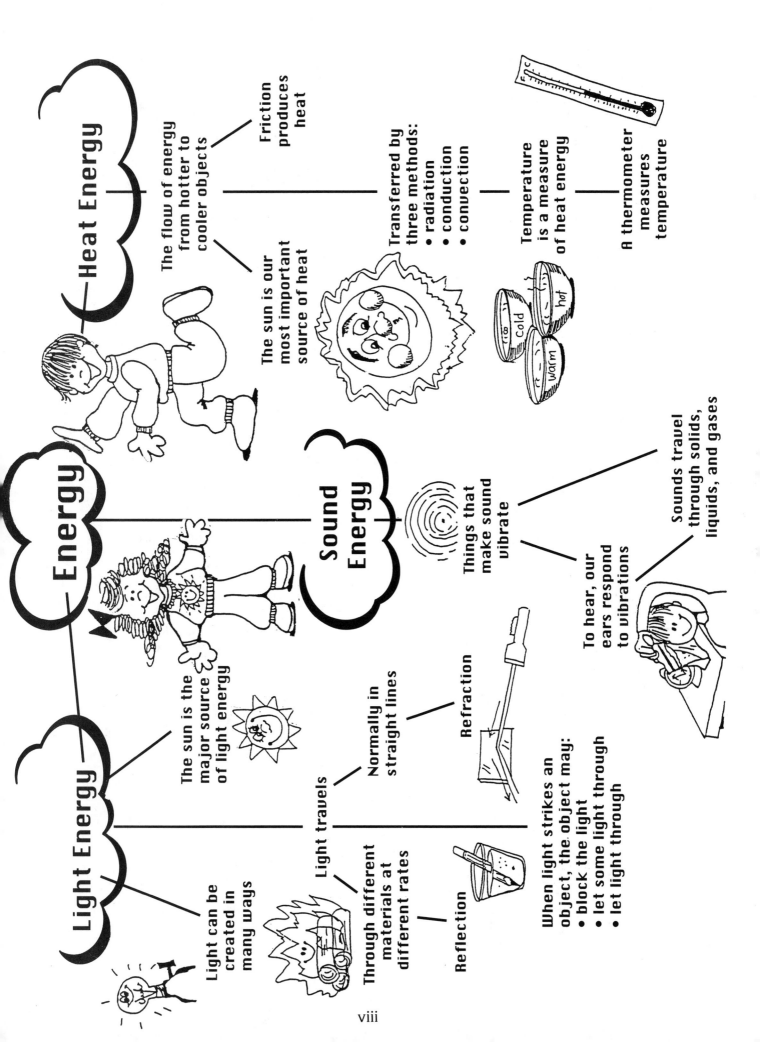

Energy

Heat Energy

The flow of energy from hotter to cooler objects

Friction produces heat

The sun is our most important source of heat

Transferred by three methods:
• radiation
• conduction
• convection

Temperature is a measure of heat energy

A thermometer measures temperature

Cold   hot   warm

Sound Energy

Things that make sound vibrate

Sounds travel through solids, liquids, and gases

To hear, our ears respond to vibrations

Light Energy

The sun is the major source of light energy

Light travels

Normally in straight lines

Refraction

Light can be created in many ways

Through different materials at different rates

Reflection

When light strikes an object, the object may:
• block the light
• let some light through
• let light through

Materials List

CONSUMABLE ITEMS

____ popsicle sticks
____ glass jar

____ thread
____ shoe box

____ transparent tape
____ newspaper

____ zipper-type plastic bags
____ paper clips

____ water
____ glass bottles

____ paper cups
____ plastic eggs

____ heavy string
____ egg carton

____ food coloring (red, blue, yellow)
____ items for eggs–rice, key, marshmallow,
    beans, cotton balls, dice, marbles,
    paper clips, pennies, toothpicks,
    macaroni, thread

____ large chart paper
____ Teddy Bear Counters

____ glue
____ construction paper

____ small mirrors
____ balloon

____ crayons
____ magazine pictures

____ hand lenses
____ stickers (happy face)

____ cellophane (red, blue, yellow)
____ flashlight

____ paper towels
____ items to test for light–
    glass jar or window pane, white paper,
    piece of transparency film, card-
    board, aluminum foil, waxed paper,
    glass of water, mirror, tissue paper

____ ice cubes
____ paper plates

____ candles
____ liquid detergent

____ plastic cups
____ prism

NON-CONSUMABLE ITEMS

____ leaves
____ wooden rulers

____ pennies
____ tuning fork

____ bowls
____ ping pong balls

____ thermometers
____ rubber bands

____ scissors
____ clear glass pan

____ Styrofoam cups
____ overhead projector

____ large jar or aquarium
____ cork

____ baby food jars
____ Slinky

____ metal rod (metal knitting needle, metal
    clothes hanger)
____ wind-up clock

____ metal can
____ thumbtacks

____ paper bag
____ metal spoon

____ plastic spoon
____ wooden spoon or stick

____ frozen juice can
____ flat plate

____ large plastic bowl
____ materials for instruments

(see *Instrument Ideas*)

Table of Contents

What is Energy?

What is energy? It is not matter; it does not have mass. You cannot hold it in your hand. Objects have energy and can gain energy from or lose energy to other objects. A moving car has energy, a pot of water heating on a burner is gaining energy from the burner, a bowling ball loses energy as it hits the pins. Energy can be bought and sold: someone pays for the electrical energy to light this classroom and for the food energy you need to run and play at recess. Energy appears in many forms including heat, light, sound, nuclear, and geothermal. Though each form is different, they are all the same in the fact that one form of energy can change into another.

Most of the energy used on earth comes from the sun. Sunlight is absorbed by the air, water, and other objects. Sunlight provides the energy green plants use to make food. Human and animal life depend on this food to provide energy to operate their bodies and muscles.

Let's look at three forms of energy: light, heat, and sound. We can see light, feel heat, and hear sound. We can also explore the way these forms of energy change into one another.

Heat energy is the random motion of molecules. Molecules in matter are always in motion, but the hotter something is the faster the molecules move. Temperature is a measure of that motion.

Sound waves carry energy through air (or other materials) as the molecules in them are pushed and pulled by a vibrating source. All sounds begin when something vibrates.

Energy is carried in light waves. Most objects do not emit visible light but reflect from other sources. Our primary source of light is the sun.

The total amount of energy in a closed system does not change. Energy can be changed from one form to another, but excluding nuclear processes, it can never be created or destroyed. This is known as the law of conservation of energy. In nuclear processes, energy can be converted into matter and matter can be converted into energy. The total amount of mass and energy does not change.

Sound Energy

Sounds are all around us. We hear the wind moving through trees, the honking of car horns, friends laughing, music playing, and countless other sounds. Sounds never stop, not even when we sleep.

All sounds we hear have one thing in common. Sound is produced by objects vibrating back and forth which make sound waves. These vibrations are transmitted to anything the vibrating object touches, including air. The waves go out in every direction so that if you could see them, they would look like concentric rounded shapes spreading out from the source, like ripples that spread out when a pebble is dropped in a pond. Plucking the strings of a guitar causes its body to vibrate. The wooden guitar body pushes nearby air molecules back and forth; most of the sound we hear comes from air pushed in and out of the hole in the center of the guitar. The disturbed air molecules push against neighboring molecules, disturbing them and so forth. The molecules do not move very far, but the energy travels away from the strings at the speed of sound.

Sound travels through solids, liquids, and gases at different speeds. It travels about 350 meters (1,129 feet) per second through air, 1500 meters (4,794 feet) per second through water, and 4,500 meters (12,620 feet) per second through wood. Sound cannot travel through an absolute vacuum because there is nothing there to vibrate.

The sense of hearing involves the outer ear, ear drum, the three tiny bones, a special snail shell-shaped chamber, the auditory nerve, and the brain. The outer ear picks up sound waves and transfers vibrations through the ear canal to the eardrum where it passes to three tiny bones that stimulate nerve cells. The auditory nerve carries the electrical impulses to the brain where it is interpreted as sound.

Sounds can be high or low. The difference in the highness or lowness of sound is called pitch. Pitch depends on the frequency of vibration of the sound source. If an object vibrates very rapidly, the ear will receive many vibrations per second, and the brain will interpret it as a high pitch. The higher the number of vibrations per second, the higher the pitch. Humans can hear vibrations between 20 and 20,000 vibrations per second. Sounds of higher frequency can be heard by animals such as dogs, bats, dolphins, and whales. The intensity or loudness of a sound depends on the amount of energy it contains.

Sound is Vibration

Topic
Sound

Key Question
How is sound made?

Focus
The students will learn that vibrating objects produce sounds and cause vibrations in whatever they touch.

Guiding Documents
Project 2061 Benchmarks
- *People can often learn about things around them by just observing those things carefully, but sometimes they can learn more by doing something to the things and noting what happens.*
- *Things that make sound vibrate.*

Science
Physical science
    sound

Integrated Processes
Observing
Communicating
Collecting and recording data
Predicting
Drawing conclusions
Interpreting data
Comparing and contrasting

Materials
Wooden rulers
Tuning forks
Popsicle sticks
Ping pong ball
Thread and tape
Rubber band
Pencil
Glass of water
Butcher paper

Background Information
Energy must by used to produce sound. Whether it is the plucking of the strings of a guitar, the striking of a drum, or the blowing of a trumpet, energy is involved. The energy causes the object to vibrate, producing sound.

Whenever a sound is produced, something is quivering, throbbing, vibrating. Such movements are the basis of the sound we hear. Sound vibrations can be something we see, like a violin string vibrating; or it can be something we feel like the vibration of a person's vocal cords; or it can be something we hear, like a ticking clock. All sounds can be traced to a vibration of some material.

In order for a sound to be heard, the vibrating material must move back and forth at least 16 times per second. The vibrating materials may be a solid, liquid, or gas.

Management
1. Attach a 12" piece of thread to the ping pong ball.
2. Wrap the rubber band around the ruler lengthwise and push a pencil underneath the rubber band.
3. Have a large chart of butcher paper to record the students' observations.

Procedure
1. Begin by asking the students to close their eyes. Have them listen to all the sounds around them. Encourage them to describe the sounds they hear and judge whether the sound is high or low, etc. Record their observations on a large chart. Go outdoors and listen to sounds.
2. Upon returning to the classroom, distribute *Listen to Sounds* and ask students to record the indoor and outdoor sounds they heard.
3. Discuss that all sound is produced by vibrations that make sound waves.

4. Use a ruler to produce a vibration by placing the ruler on a desk so one end sticks out over the edge. Pluck the ruler with a finger as you hold the other end tightly against the desk.
5. Shorten the amount of ruler sticking out and pluck the ruler again. Ask the students if there is a difference in

sound. When you make the ruler shorter, is there a change in sound? [Yes, the pitch is higher.]

6. Tell the students to clench a popsicle stick between their teeth. Have them pluck the end sticking out and listen to the vibrations. Ask if they can feel the vibrations?

7. Vibrations can also be demonstrated by striking a tuning fork on a soft shoe or with a rubber mallet and touching a ping pong ball that is hanging by a thread. (The vibration from the tuning fork will kick the ping pong ball away.) Yet another way to demonstrate the vibrations from the tuning fork is to gently touch the vibrating tines to the surface of water in a glass.

8. Demonstrate that vibrations cannot only be seen, but can be felt. Have the students place their hands flat on their desks; move around the room with a vibrating tuning fork and touch the handle to the desk of each child. Ask the students what they feel.

9. Make a one-string ukulele by wrapping a rubber band lengthwise around a ruler. Push a pencil underneath and perpendicular to the rubber band. Pluck the rubber band. Move the pencil and pluck again in the same place. Listen to the change in sound and watch how the rubber band vibrates.

10. Demonstrate how the loudness depends on the amount the ukulele string is pulled aside in plucking.

11. Do worksheet *Sound is Vibration*.

Discussion

1. What do all sounds have in common? [vibrations, vibrating sources, traveling energy]

2. What do vibrating objects look like? [objects moving back and forth rapidly, blurry]

3. What do vibrations feel like? [tingly, wiggly, etc.]

4. Describe the change in the sound when you move the pencil and change the length of the rubber band. (The sound becomes higher or lower. The rubber band vibrations are different.)

5. What caused the ping pong ball to bounce away from the tuning fork? [rapid back and forth movements of the tines of the tuning fork]

Extensions

1. Have the students use the lists of sounds they made to create a poem. For example, the form of the poem could be

SOUNDS

I hear   children giggling,
           cars honking,
           leaves rustling,
           people singing,
           special sounds

                    with my ears.

2. Have the students remember sounds that they enjoy hearing. List their responses on a chart labeled "I Like to Hear . . . ." Have them remember sounds that they do not like to hear and add those to the list under "I Do Not Like to Hear . . . ." Later categorize the list into high, low; loud, soft sounds.

3. Brainstorm some important sounds and how people should react to them. [fire alarm, fire engine and ambulance siren, school bell, smoke detector alarm, teacher's or police officer's whistle]

Listen to Sounds

1. Close your eyes and get very quiet. Listen to all the sounds you can hear in one minute.

2. Open your eyes. Make a list of the sounds you heard.

Indoor Sounds

1._____	7._____
2._____	8._____
3._____	9._____
4._____	10._____
5._____	11._____
6._____	12._____

3. Go outside and sit quietly. Shut your eyes and listen for at least 1 minute. Open your eyes and make a list of the sounds you heard.

Outdoor Sounds

1._____	7._____
2._____	8._____
3._____	9._____
4._____	10._____
5._____	11._____
6._____	12._____

How were the sounds alike?_____

How were the sounds different?_____

PRIMARILY PHYSICS   5   © 1994 AIMS Education Foundation

Sound is Vibration

You will Need: Tuning fork 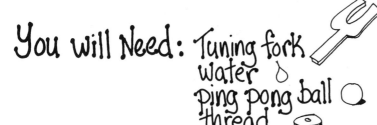 tape
water ô ruler
ping pong ball ○ rubber band
thread pencil

Do This:

1. Hold one edge of a ruler tightly on your desk. Pluck the other end of the ruler lightly. Listen. Make the ruler shorter. Make the ruler longer.

2. Clench a craft stick with your teeth. Pluck the end of the stick and listen. Change the length and try again.

3. Strike a tuning fork on your shoe (or hand) Watch and listen. Put the vibrating tuning fork in water. Watch.

    Put a ping pong ball on a thread. Touch the ball with a vibrating tuning fork. Watch.

   Touch your desk with a vibrating tuning fork. Feel.

4. Make a mini-ukulele. Wrap a rubber band around a ruler. Push a pencil under the rubber band. Pluck the rubber band. Watch and listen. Move the pencil and try again.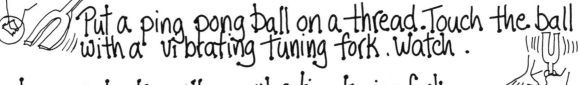

5. How are all these activities alike?_____

6   © 1994 AIMS Education Foundation

Traveling Sounds

Topic
Sounds

Key Question
Can sounds travel through solids, liquids, and gas?

Focus
The students will be able to explain that sounds travel through air, water, and wood.

Guiding Documents
Project 2061 Benchmarks
- *People can often learn about things around them by just observing those things carefully, but sometimes they can learn more by doing something to the things and noting what happens.*
- *Things that make sound vibrate.*
- *People use their senses to find out about their surroundings and themselves. Different senses give different information. Sometimes a person can get different information about the same thing by moving closer to it or further away from it.*

Science
Physical science
  sound energy

Integrated Processes
Observing
Comparing and contrasting
Communicating
Predicting
Drawing conclusions

Materials
Wind-up clock
Large zipper-type plastic bag
Water
Table top
Empty metal coffee can
Paper bag
Glass jar
Shoe box
Old newspaper

Background Information
Sound waves travel through every kind of material; but sound cannot travel through a vacuum because there is nothing to vibrate.

Solids, liquids, and gases all conduct sound, but the speed of sound is different for each type of material. Most sounds that we hear are transmitted through air. Sound waves travel much faster through solids and liquids than through gases because the molecules of solids and liquids are closer together.

Sample speeds:

Air	330 meters/second —	129 feet/sec.
Water.	1500 meters/second —	4794 feet/sec.
Wood.	4500 meters/second —	14850 feet/sec.
Metal.	5000 meters/second —	16500 feet/sec.

Management
1. Fill the plastic bag with water and seal tightly.
2. Collect a coffee can, paper bag, glass jar, and shoe box with newspaper. They must be large enough to put the clock inside.
3. If a wind-up clock that ticks is not available, use a music box or hit two spoons together.

Procedure
1. Wind the clock. Have the students close their eyes and listen to the clock ticking. (See activity sheet *Traveling Sounds.*

2. Have students raise their hands if they can hear the ticking. Ask, "What is the sound traveling through?"
3. Explain that the air is a gas. Sound is produced by vibrations of the clock disturbing the air.
4. Have the students press their ears against a wood surface (table top, desk, wooden floor) and place the clock on the table top some distance from the student's ears. Ask, "Can you hear the sound?" "Is the sound louder or softer than when you heard it through air?" [louder because the path between molecules is shorter]
5. Have a student hold the water-filled bag to his/her ear. Hold the clock against the other side of the bag. Ask the student, "Can you hear the clock ticking?" [Yes]

6. Put the clock inside of the following: a metal can, paper bag, glass jar, and a shoe box stuffed with newspaper. Have the students tell when the sound was the loudest and when it was softest. Which container(s) did the clock make vibrate the best?

7. Try having the students press their ear against a metal surface (metal cabinet, metal door, or metal ruler) and put the clock on the metal surface. "Does sound travel through metal?" [Yes!]

Discussion

1. Of the items supplied, which ones conduct sound? [All]

2. Which materials (supplied) seemed to make the sound softer? [shoe box with newspapers because they absorbed sound energy] Which seemed to make the sound louder? [wood and metal because they provide a direct path to your ear]

Extensions

1. Take the students outside and have them press one of their ears to the earth. Bounce a ball or stomp your feet at least ten feet away. Ask them if they heard you. Explain that the Native Americans used this method to hear approaching people or herds of animals. They could feel the vibrations through the earth before they could hear them through the air.

2. Have the **students** think of some different articles that sound can **travel** through and test each one. Do the activity page *What Can Sound Travel Through?* as a homework assignment.

3. Bend the ends of a metal clothes hanger so that you can hold them to the outside of your ears with your fingers. Have someone tap the hanger *lightly* with a pencil. Listen while someone else tries it. Why does it sound so loud when you do it and so soft when someone else tries it? [The vibrations go straight to your ears when you do it, and through the air when someone else does it.]

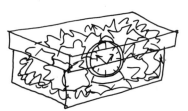

Traveling Sounds

Name

You Will Need: 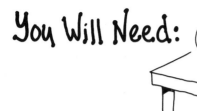 wind up clock
large plastic bag
of water
table
metal can   paper bag
glass jar
shoe box
newspaper

Do This:

1. Listen to the clock. The sound is traveling through air.

2. Put the clock on a table. Press your ear to the table. The sound is traveling through wood.

3. Fill a plastic bag with water. Listen to the clock through it. The sound is traveling through water and plastic.

When was sound the loudest? Why?

1. air

2. wood

3. water

4. Put the clock inside a metal can, paper bag, glass jar, and a shoebox with newspaper.

When was the sound softest? Why?

metal can

paper bag

glass jar

shoe box with
newspaper

What Can Sound Travel Through?

Name

Make a list of your predictions. Test each one. Then make a new list of things you found that sound could travel through.

I think that sound can travel through these things.

I plan to test my predictions by _____

_____

I found out that sound travels through these things.

Paper Cup Telephone

Topic
Sound

Key Question
How can we use string to conduct sound?

Focus
The students will be able to demonstrate that sound travels through solids.

Guiding Documents
Project 2061 Benchmarks
- *People can often learn about things around them by just observing those things carefully, but sometimes they can learn more by doing something to the things and noting what happens.*
- *Everybody can do science and invent things and ideas*
- *Raise questions about the world around them and be willing to seek answers to some of them by making careful observations and trying things out.*

Science
Physical science
  sound

Processes
Observing
Comparing and contrasting
Communicating
Drawing conclusions

Materials
For each telephone:
  paper cups
  6 meters string
  sharp pencil
  2 paper clips

Background Information
This activity is an effective way to show that sound wave energy can be conducted through a stretched string better than through open air. The vibrating string can carry sound, and, when the vibration is stopped, the sound is stopped.

If we hear someone talking in the next room when all the doors are closed, we are hearing sound that has probably traveled through air and then through the wall and then through the air of the room we are in.

Management
1. This activity works well with students grouped in pairs or groups of four.
2. Prior to the activity, cut and distribute the string to each group.

Procedure
1. In introducing this activity, ask the students how they can make string conduct sound. Record these ideas on the chalkboard or overhead projector.
2. Allow students time to explore their ideas and to share their results with the class.
3. Tell them that they are going to use the string to make a paper cup telephone that will conduct sounds.
4. Distribute the rest of the supplies.
5. Have students make a small hole in the center of the bottom of each cup with a pencil.
6. Tie one end of the string to a paper clip and thread the other end through the inside of the cup and out the hole. The paper clip will prevent the string from being pulled out of the cup.
7. Thread the end of the string down through the hole in the bottom of the second cup. Reaching into the cup pull the end of the string far enough to attach the other paper clip.
8. Inform the students that this completes the end of their paper cup telephones. Their next task is to discover how to operate them.
9. After a period of investigation time, students should come to the realization that one student talks into one cup while another student hold the other cup over his/her ear. The string must be taut!

car phones

10. If necessary, explain that when one person speaks into the cup, the sound travels in waves along the string and makes the other cup vibrate, too. This is how sound travels between the cups.
11. To explore the tautness of the string variable, have the students let the string go slack. What happens to the sound? [Becomes fainter with reduced tension.]
12. Try *Slinky Sound*. Does it sound different from the paper cup phone?

Discussion
1. What did you have to do in order to hear your partner's voice? [stretch the string tight and speak into the cup]
2. What is transmitting the sound from the cup? [the string]
3. Could you see the string vibrate while talking?[no]
4. Think of ways or adaptations for using this telephone.
5. Tell me in your own words what you learned from this activity.

Extensions
1. Make a phone tap by crossing one set of phone lines over another. One string must be looped over the string it crosses.
2. Have the students find out the maximum length the string can be and still be able to hear someone talking.
3. Try using some other material such as wire, heavier rope, yarn, roving, etc., to see which one conducts the vibrations the best.
4. Construct the lion by following the instructions on the activity page and see if the children can make it roar by moving their fingers along the string. (It may help to dampen the string.) Can you think of any other animal sound you can make?
5. Lead the class in a discussion about how their lives would be different if we didn't have telephones for communication.
6. Use the touch-tone pad or the telephone dial as a code for making and solving math problems.

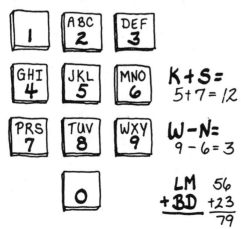

Slinky® Sound

Name

You Will Need:

2 paper cups
1 meter of string
2 paper clips
1 toy metal slinky®

Do This:

1. Make a hole in the bottom of each cup.

2. Cut the string in half. Insert one end of each string into each of the cups.

3. Tie each string to a paper clip inside each cup.

4. Stretch the slinky® to about 2 meters in length.

5. Tie the end of one of the strings to the slinky.® Tie the other string near the first one.

6. Put both cups to your ears. Have a partner pluck one end of the slinky.

7. Listen! What does it sound like to you?

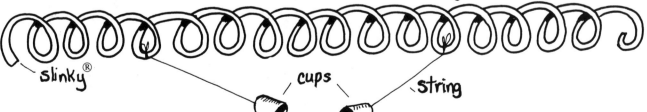

slinky®   cups   string

8. Try a coat hanger, fork, or spoon.

© 1994 AIMS Education Foundation

Cut out this circle and push cup through.

3. Pull down the length of the string with your fingernails to make the lion roar.

1. Cut out lion and glue on tagboard.
2. Tie string to a paper clip. Pass string through the hole in the bottom of the cup.

MY STYRO-PHONE

My Styro-phone is a wondrous thing
I can talk to my friend at the end of my string
Just by whispering a word in my cup.
I can hear every word without turning it up!
by Karen Adler

Musical Bottle Xylophone

Topic
Sound

Key Question
How do different amounts of water affect the sound made by tapping the bottles?

Focus
When glass bottles filled with different levels of water are tapped, students will be able to hear a difference in sound.

Math
Graphing

Guiding Documents
Project 2061 Benchmarks
- *People can often learn about things around them by just observing those things carefully, but sometimes they can learn more by doing something to the things and noting what happens.*
- *Everybody can do science and invent things and ideas.*
- *Simple graphs can help to tell about observations.*

Science
Physical science
  sound

Integrated Processes
Observing
Predicting
Communicating
Collecting and recording data
Comparing and contrasting
Drawing conclusions

Materials
Five identical glass bottles
Food coloring – red, blue, yellow, green, orange
Wall chart
Glue
6" x 18" construction paper strips
Student page
Optional: toy xylophone

Background Information
Vibrating objects produce sound by causing vibrations in whatever they touch. All sounds are made by things vibrating. Objects with more mass vibrate more slowly and have a lower sound (pitch); objects with less mass vibrate more rapidly and have a higher sound (pitch). When a bottle is tapped, the glass and the contents vibrate and make a sound. By adding different levels of water, there are differing masses to vibrate and the pitch of the sound can be changed. The bottle with the least amount of water will vibrate the fastest and have the highest pitch. The one with the most water will vibrate the slowest and have the lowest pitch.

Note that the situation is **very different** for blowing across the mouth of a bottle. In blowing, it is the **amount of air** that is set in vibration. Empty bottles have a lot of air to vibrate and have a low pitch; fuller bottles have less air and produce a higher pitch **when blown**.

Management
1. Get five glass bottles that are identical.
2. Prepare the five bottles of water, each with a different level of water.
3. Use only the three colors of food coloring – red, blue, and yellow – and let the students mix the colors to get orange and green.
4. Prepare the graph and markers for the students' predictions.

Procedure
1. If available, show the students a toy xylophone and ask them to describe it. It may be painted with different colors which students notice, but keep probing until someone observes the size differences in the metal plates. Play the xylophone to demonstrate high and low pitch. Tell them that all small objects vibrate fast and large objects vibrate slowly.
2. Place the five bottles, each with a different level of water, on the table and ask the students if the bottles will make a sound if they are hit with a pencil.
3. Put a different food coloring in each bottle.
4. Show the graph and ask the students to predict which bottle will make the highest sound or pitch. Have the students use the markers to record their prediction.

16

5. Have several students come up to test the bottles using a pencil to cause the vibration. Tap various bottles until it is clear to the students that the bottle with the most water has the lowest pitch.

6. Try blowing across the bottles to produce sound. Guide the students to realizing that the air in the bottle is vibrating. The bottle with the least air (most water) will have the highest pitch and the one with the most air (least water) will have the lowest pitch. Ah-ha, the effect is opposite to that of tapping!

7. Have the children try to tap out a song on the bottles. The teacher should do it first. Try *Twinkle, Twinkle, Little Star* or *Row, Row, Row Your Boat*.

8. Distribute the worksheets and have the children color the water in the bottles to match the colors of the water in the real bottles.

9. Hand out the strips of construction paper.

10. Have students compose a song by placing the colored bottle pictures on the construction paper strip in the order they want them played.

11. Have the students play their songs for the class. Allow them to first tap the bottles to play the tune and then to blow into them.

Discussion

1. Which bottle had the highest sound when it was struck?...blown into?

2. Which bottle had the lowest sound when it was struck?...blown into?

3. Why did the bottle with the least water have the highest pitch when struck and the lowest pitch when blown across? [The glass and water were vibrating when the bottle was struck and the air was vibrating when blown.]

4. Which way did you like your song played, tapping or blowing?

5. What other things do you know that make sounds in this manner?

Extensions

1. Estimate the number of millimeters of water in a full bottle. (Measure the number of millimeters in a paper cup, estimate the number of filled paper cups, and add (or multiply) to get the estimate.) What amount is printed on the bottle? Why is there a difference? (Bottles are never filled to the top to allow for expansion in hot weather.)

2. Put some other material in the bottles (sand, Jello™, beans). Does it sound the same?

3. Listen to music with your eyes closed, then draw what you see.

4. Use the graph for math drills. Ask questions like:
   – How many voted for blue?
   – How many voted for red?
   – How many more voted for red than _____?
   – If I add blue, red, and green votes, how many do I have in all?
   – How many more people voted for red than green?

5. The concept of pitch can be further developed by using the stories *Goldilocks and the Three Bears, Little Red Riding Hood,* and *The Three Billy Goats Gruff*. The children can act out the pitch changes for the main characters.

Prediction Graph

						blue.
						green.
						yellow
						orange
						red

Musical Bottle Xylophone

Color, cut out, and glue on pattern strips to make songs. Play your music for an audience.

red   orange   yellow   green   blue.

Sound of Voices

Topic
Vibrations of vocal cords

Key Question
How is the sound of the human voice made?

Focus
The students will be able to explain that sound is produced by the vocal cords of the body.

Guiding Documents
Project 2061 Benchmarks
- *People can often learn about things around them by just observing those things carefully, but sometimes they can learn more by doing something to the things and noting what happens.*
- *Things that make sound vibrate.*

Science
Physical science
　sounds

Integrated Processes
Observing
Comparing and contrasting
Communicating
Predicting

Materials
Balloon

Background Information
　The human voice is produced in the larynx. The vocal cords, two small folds of tissue, stretch across the vocal tract. As air from the lungs rushes past the vocal cords, they vibrate, producing sound.

　This activity will give the students an idea of how their vocal cords work. The air in the balloon represents the air that you use to talk. The mouth of the balloon represents your vocal cords which vibrate as the air passes to make sounds. Your throat, mouth, and nose act as resonators to "shape" the raw sound into speech.

Management
1. Get a large balloon if you can; it holds more air.
2. The teacher could read some or all of the page *Voice Box Reader's Theater* to the students.

Procedure
1. Have students put their hands on their throats and hum. What do they feel?
2. Where are the vibrations coming from? [your vocal cords]
3. How do your vocal cords make sounds? [your vocal cords vibrate to make voice sounds]
4. Inflate the balloon.
5. Grasp each side of the neck of the balloon with the thumb and forefinger of each hand.
6. As the air escapes from the balloon, pull on each side of the balloon. What happens as the rubber vibrates? [it produces a sound]
7. Stretch the mouth of the balloon even more and let some of the air out of it. As the rubber is pulled tighter, what happens? [the pitch of the sound gets higher]

Discussion
1. You make voice sounds when you breathe out. Can you make the same sound breathing in? Try it.
2. Can you whistle while breathing in? Try it; is it easy?
3. What part of the human throat does the stretched mouth of the balloon represent? [vocal cords]
4. What does the air in the balloon represent? [the air in our lungs]
5. Are your vocal cords vibrating when you whisper?
6. What happens when we pull the neck of the balloon real tight? [it makes a high pitch] Try to make your vocal cords real tight and produce a sound. What kind of sound do you make? [high]
7. What happens when the neck of the balloon is pulled loosely? What kind of sound can you produce with looser vocal cords?

Extension
1. Have the students make a list of words to describe sounds people make. Examples are talking, speaking, yelling, coughing, singing, crying, laughing, giggling, whispering.
2. Perform the *Voice Box Reader's Theater*. Individuals or small groups say the first nine lines, then the whole group joins in on the final two lines.

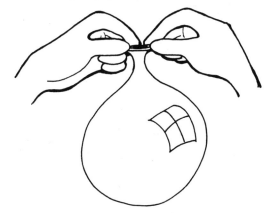

Voice Box

When you breathe normally, the air goes through your nose into your windpipe. The windpipe is a hollow tube leading from the back of your throat towards the lungs. At the top of the windpipe is a hollow organ called the voice box or larynx. It is made of bone and cartilage held together by ligaments and muscles.

The vocal cords in your voice box are two, straight, elastic-like strings. When you are not speaking or singing, these cords are relaxed against the sides of your voice box. When you start to talk or sing, tiny muscles bring the vocal cords closer together. Air coming up from the lungs makes the vocal cords move back and forth very fast (vibrate). When vocal cords vibrate, sounds are produced. Stretching the vocal cords tight and thin makes your voice high and squeaky. Relaxing them to a loose and wide shape makes low, deep sounds.

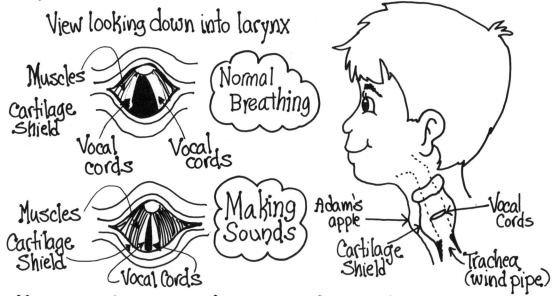

View looking down into larynx

Muscles
Cartilage Shield
Vocal cords   Vocal cords

Normal Breathing

Muscles
Cartilage Shield
Vocal Cords

Making Sounds

Adam's apple
Cartilage Shield
Vocal Cords
Trachea (wind pipe)

You can find your larynx just behind the bump in your throat called the Adam's apple. Feel around for the cartilage shield. The larynx is right behind it. Put your hand on your larynx and hum or talk. Feel the vibrations. Make the lowest sound that you can. Now make the highest sound. Feel the muscles move.

Voice Box

Readers' Theater

I can whisper. (Can you hear me?)

I can shout. (Hey! Throw me the ball!)

I can hum when I'm about. (hmmmmm)

I can laugh. (ha, ha, hee, hee, ho, ho)

I can sing. (la, la, la, la, la, la, la)

I can sob when I'm crying. (boo hoo)

I can yodel. (yo de lay hee hooo)

I can talk. (Could I have another cookie please?)

I can giggle when I walk. (tee, hee.)

All these sounds my voice box makes.
(point to larynx)

I use them all to communicate.
(all turn to each other and begin talking)

by
Chris & Sheryl
Mercier

Eggs-Full of SOUND

Topic
Sounds

Key Question
Can you identify objects by the various sounds they make?

Focus
The students will be able to identify objects by the sounds they make.

Guiding Documents
Project 2061 Benchmarks
- *People can often learn about things around them by just observing those things carefully, but sometimes they can learn more by doing something to the things and noting what happens.*
- *People use their sense to find out about their surroundings and themselves. Different senses give different information. Sometimes a person can get different information about the same thing by moving closer to it or further away from it.*
- *When people give different descriptions of the same thing, it is usually a good idea to make some fresh observations instead of just arguing about who is right.*

Science
Physical science
    sound
Life science
    human senses
      hearing

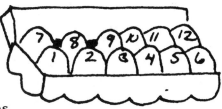

Integrated Processes
Observing
Communicating
Collecting and recording data
Predicting
Drawing conclusions

Materials
12 plastic eggs
Egg carton
Items for eggs: marshmallows, rice, beans, pins, cotton, dice, paper clips, key, marbles, bottle cap, pennies, toothpicks, macaroni, spool of thread.

Background Information
We have all learned to identify different things by the sounds they make even if we do not see them, i.e., a motorcycle, a door closing, money jingling, water running.

This activity will give the students a chance to identify some very common items by the sounds they make.

Management
1. Get a dozen plastic eggs, usually available in a toy store. If eggs are not available, substitute with film canisters or margarine tubs.
2. Number each egg.
3. Place the items in the plastic eggs.
4. Put the eggs in the egg carton in any order.

Procedure
1. Discuss with the students various sounds that they can recognize without seeing (a pencil that has been dropped, keys that are rattled, a book as it is being closed).
2. Ask students to close their eyes. Make some noises and have the students try to identify the sounds.
3. Tell the students that they are to listen to the sounds made by the objects in the eggs as you shake them. Have them predict what the objects are.
4. Shake each egg and have the students listen. Have the students record their predictions by cutting out the pictures and laying them on the pictures of the numbered eggs.
5. Open the eggs and show the students the contents. They may move any incorrect predictions and glue the actual pictured objects on the appropriately numbered egg.

Discussion
1. Which objects made loud sounds?
2. Which objects made soft sounds?
3. Did any egg sound empty? Why do you think this happened?
4. Which objects are the easiest to identify? Why?
5. Were there any objects that were very difficult to identify?

6. Why do you think it is important to recognize and understand sounds? [for our safety, to understand language, to recognize friends]
7. If you were to fill the eggs with your own objects, what would you choose?

Extensions
1. Fill pairs of eggs with the same objects. Have the students match the pairs of eggs by their sounds.
2. Send an egg home, have parents fill the egg with mystery objects and return to school. Allow the class to guess the objects by the sounds they make.
3. Hide beans inside an egg. Shake the egg. Have the students guess the number of beans hidden inside by the sound they make. Record their guesses on an egg-shaped wall chart. Ask questions like: Which guess is closest to 100?...50?...25? What is the highest guess? What is the lowest? Open the egg and count the objects. Repeat with a different number of beans.
4. Discuss sounds that warns us of danger, such as car horns, bells, sirens, or police cars, fire engines, ambulances, bells at train crossings and so on.

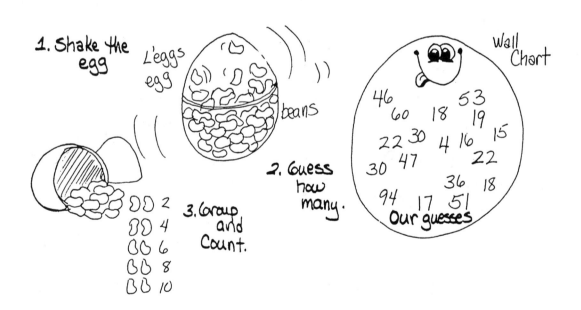

Eggs-Full of Sound

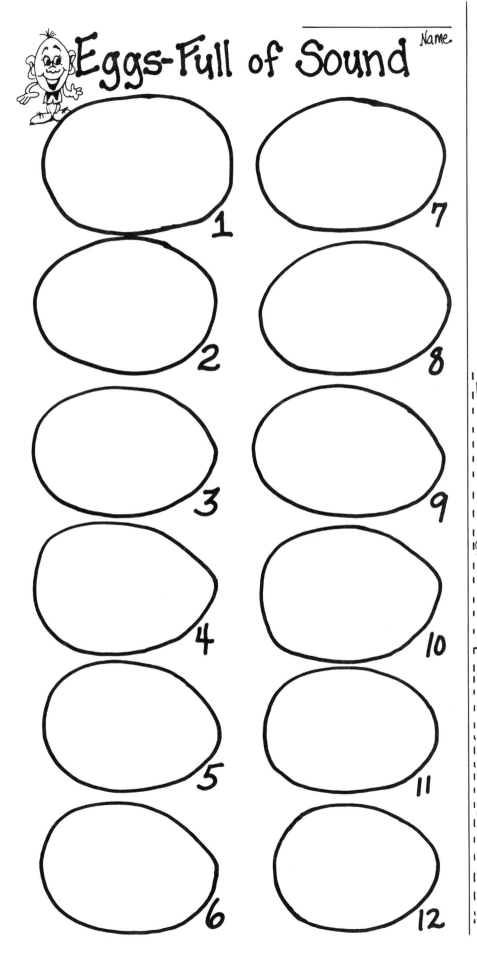

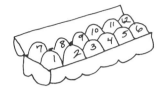

1. Cut out the pictures.
2. Shake each mystery egg and listen.
3. Guess what is inside and put its picture on the numbered egg.
4. Open the eggs and glue the pictures to show each sound.

marshmallows   rice
beans   toothpicks
thread   cotton
dice   paper clips
key   marbles
pennies   macaroni

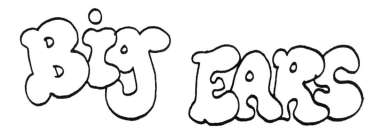 

"Big Ears"

Topic
Sound

Key Question
How do our ears allow us to hear sounds?

Focus
The children will be able to explain that the ear is the organ of the body that receives sound.

Guiding Documents
Project 2061 Benchmarks
- *People can often learn about things around them by just observing those things carefully, but sometimes they can learn more by doing something to things and noting what happens.*
- *People use their senses to find out about their surroundings and themselves. Different senses give different information. Sometimes a person can get different information about the same thing by moving closer to it or further away from it.*

Science
Physical science
    sound
Life science
    hearing

Integrated Processes
Observing
Communicating
Predicting
Drawing conclusions

Materials
Paper to make a megaphone

Background Information
We hear because our ears respond to vibrations in the air. The important parts involved in hearing are protected inside the skull. The **outer ear** that we see plays only a small part in hearing. Its shape helps direct air vibrations into the ear canal. The air vibrations hit the eardrum – a flexible membrane inside the ear canal – and cause it to vibrate. The vibrating eardrum causes movement in three tiny bones (the hammer, anvil and stirrup) in a chamber called the **middle ear**. Then the vibration is sent on into the **inner ear**. The inner ear is composed of the cochlea and the semicircular canals. The sound waves exert pressure on fluid in the cochlea where the fluid's movement is detected by the tiny hairs connected to the auditory nerve. Electrical impulses travel up the auditory nerve to the brain where they are identified as sounds.

Behind the eardrum is a tube, the *eustachian tube*, which connects the middle ear to the throat. Its purpose is to equalize the air pressure on both sides of the ear drum.

The semicircular canal in the inner ear is the sense organ for balance.

Management
CAUTION the students that loud sounds and sharp objects can damage the ear.

Procedure
1. Discuss why ears are important. (They allow us to hear and communicate. The ear is sensitive to a wide range of sounds – high, low, loud, and soft.)
2. Discuss with the students the different parts of the ear (see *Background Information*). [The outer ear (the part we see) and the ear drum, the middle ear with the chain of three bones, and the inner ear with the cochlea.]
3. Have the students fill in the blanks with the names for the parts of the ear on the *My Ear* activity sheet.
4. Have the students listen to the sounds from a tape or record. Begin with the volume off, slowly turn the volume higher and have the students raise their hands when they are able to hear the music. When all hands are raised slowly turn the volume down until only a few hands are still up.
5. Tell the class that there is another way to "turn the volume up." Show them how to make "big ears" by putting their hands behind their ears with their palms facing outward. Have them make big ears and compare the number of students who can hear the music.
6. Set the volume of the tape so that all students can hear. Have them listen, alternately with their "big ears" off and on. Ask them to describe the difference in the sound. They should notice that by making their outer ear "larger," they are able to "catch" more sound and it sounds differently.

7. Explain that the ear can pick up very soft sounds and is very sensitive. Loud sounds with much energy can cause pain and damage to the ear. The hammer, anvil, and stirrup respond much less efficiently to loud sounds (they slip) protecting the delicate hair cells of the inner ear.

Discussion
1. What do your hands catch when you make "big ears?" [sound vibrations]
2. Why do some animals (rabbits and elephants) need to have big ears? [Their eyesight is poor, so they rely on their keen hearing.]

Extensions
1. Make two megaphones. Have the students go out on the baseball diamond with one standing on home plate and the other standing on the pitcher's mound. Ask them to talk to each other (without yelling) with the megaphones. Does the sound carry? Megaphones permit sound to go out only in one direction. Thus energy is concentrated rather than being dissipated over a wide space.
2. Discuss noise pollution. Ask the class how loud noises make them feel. For example, can they work well when the class is noisy? Does a loud motor-cycle sound bother them?
3. Take a listening walk. The children can apply the "big ears" technique to help them hear. Prepare the children to listen to sounds during their walk. Take a small tape recorder along. Back in the classroom, discuss what they heard and what made those sounds. Categorize the sounds into loud, soft; high, low; near, far; people, animals, weather; if they liked or disliked the sounds, etc.

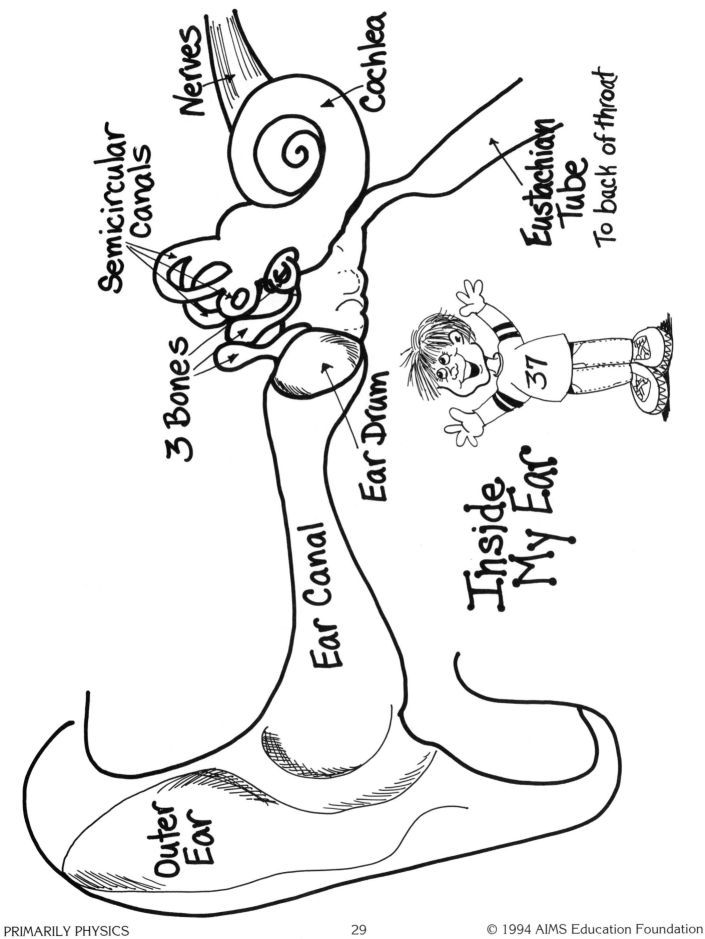

Nerves

Cochlea

Semicircular Canals

Eustachian Tube

To back of throat

3 Bones

Ear Drum

Inside My Ear

37

Ear Canal

Outer Ear

Inside My Ear

Topic
Sound energy

Key Question
Are two ears better than one to locate the source of sounds?

Focus
The students will test to see if two ears are better than one for locating sound.

Guiding Documents
Project 2061 Benchmarks
- *People can often learn about things around them by just observing those things carefully, but sometimes they can learn more by doing something to the things and noting what happens.*
- *People use their senses to find out about their surroundings and themselves. Different senses give different information. Sometimes a person can get different information about the same thing by moving closer to it or further away from it.*

Science
Physical science
    sound energy

Integrated Processes
Observing
Predicting
Communicating
Collecting and recording data
Interpreting data
Drawing conclusions

Materials
Pencils (see *Management*)

Background Information
    The sense of hearing involves the ear, the auditory nerve, and a special center within the brain. The outer ear, shaped like a funnel, picks up sound waves and leads them to the ear canal. At the inner end of the ear canal is a thin membrane called the eardrum. As sound waves strike the eardrum, they cause the eardrum to vibrate. The eardrum passes on the vibration to three tiny bones. These three bones carry the vibrations to the inner ear. The inner ear has many small hair cells which receive the vibrations. These cells connect with the auditory nerve which carries the sound message to the brain.

    Our brain uses messages from both ears to locate the direction from which a sound comes. The head blocks sound waves so that one ear receives them directly and the other ear slightly later and weaker after they go around the head. Only a sound from straight ahead, straight behind or directly above or below our head will sound the same in both ears.

    The distance a sound source is away from us is usually detected by its loudness compared to how loud the sound normally seems.

Management
1. Have three of four students stand in various parts of the room as noisemakers. Supply them with pencils. All should make exactly the same sound. Instead of pencils, you may want to use a bell, or seeds in a cup.
2. All the rest of the students in the class will be the test subjects. They are to remain seated in their desks and close their eyes.

Procedure
1. Discuss with the students the function, form, and workings of the human ear.
2. Explain to the students that they are going to do an activity to see how the ears help us to detect sound direction.
3. Four students should be chosen to be sound makers, and they should be seated randomly around the room.
4. The rest of the students are the test subjects and also the record keepers. Instruct these students to shut their eyes and listen carefully to the sound they will hear, and be ready to point in the direction from which they think the sound originated. Distribute the worksheet *Which Way?*
5. Begin the test by having one of the noisemakers tap the pencil on the desk. (Whatever noise is chosen should be repeatable. Each sound maker should make exactly the same sound when it is his/her turn.)
6. All of the test subjects should point in the direction from which they thought the sound came and then

open their eyes. The test subjects should indicate on their worksheet under *Both Ears* whether they were correct or not.

7. Have the test subjects close their eyes again, and the teacher should silently select another noisemaker to tap a pencil to repeat the test. Randomly pick noisemakers around the room until all have produced the sound and five tries have been made.

8. Repeat the whole procedure again, but this time have the test subjects cover their left ears with their hands.

Discussion

1. When was it the hardest for you to point to the sound maker?
2. When was it the easiest for you to point to the sound maker?
3. Why are two ears better at detecting direction than one?
4. When you are covering one ear, what can you do to help you find the noisemaker? [Turn your head.]

Extensions

1. Try the test again, but test with one ear first and then with two.
2. A test could be run where the right ear is covered instead of the left.
3. Invite a health specialist, a school nurse, or a parent to speak to the class about ear care and how to test hearing.

Which Way?

Are two ears better than one to locate sounds?

Both Ears

1.	First try	yes	no
2.	Second try	yes	no
3.	Third try	yes	no
4.	Fourth try	yes	no
5.	Fifth try	yes	no

Left Ear Covered

1.	First try	yes	no
2.	Second try	yes	no
3.	Third try	yes	no
4.	Fourth try	yes	no
5.	Fifth try	yes	no

Shut your eyes. Listen for the soundmaker to make the sound. Point in the direction of the sound. Open your eyes and find the soundmaker. Mark each try that you are correct.

What did you find out? _____

_____

_____

_____

Musical Instruments

Topic
Sound

Key Question
What kind of instrument can you create that makes sounds by striking, plucking, or blowing?

Focus
The students will create instruments that they can strike, blow into, or pluck.

Guiding Documents
Project 2061 Benchmarks
- *People can often learn about things around them by just observing those things carefully, but sometimes they can learn more by doing something to the things and noting what happens.*
- *Everybody can do science and invent things and ideas.*
- *Things that make sound vibrate.*
- *People can learn from each other by telling and listening, showing and watching, and imitating what others do.*

Science
Physical science
   sound

Integrated Processes
Observing
Comparing and contrasting
Communicating
Classifying

Materials
Various throw-away items (see *Instrument Ideas*)
String
Balloons

Background Information
Sound is produced by vibrating objects. Sound waves are a series of disturbances traveling through the air where the air pressure is above normal (compression) or below normal (rarefaction). These waves go out in every direction so that, if you could see them, they would look like concentric, rounded shapes spreading out from the source of the noise. The plucking of the strings of a guitar causes those strings to vibrate. The movement of those strings pushes and pulls the air around them, thus causing disturbances in the air to travel outward from the strings. A guitar has a hollow wooden body that acts as a sounding board. When the string vibrates, the wood vibrates at the same frequency. The air inside and outside the guitar vibrates so that we can hear the musical note.

All other musical instruments cause similar waves when they vibrate. While the guitar is set into vibration by plucking a string, other instruments can be set into vibration by striking them or blowing into them.

Instruments that produce sound through striking are grouped into the percussion section of a band. Woodwinds make music through blowing, which causes a reed to set an air column into vibration. Brass instruments, like trumpets, sound when the player's vibrating lips set an air column into vibration. Strings, as the name implies, have strings to originate a sound.

Management
1. Send a letter home to parents asking them to save coffee cans, aluminum pie pans, clay flower pots, glass bottles, rubber bands, spoons, oatmeal boxes, and other items which can be used for band instruments.
2. Make two or three instruments to show to the class.

Procedure
1. Show the students several of the collected items. Ask them how they think these things could be used to make sounds.
2. Tell them they are going to use these items to make musical instruments.
3. Brainstorm with the students how various materials could be used to make an instrument.
4. Show the students two or three instruments you have made; have them identify the method by which each is played (blown, struck, or plucked). Play the instruments so the students can hear them.
5. Either in groups or singly, have the students make an instrument of their choice (see *How To Construct Musical Instruments*).
6. When the instruments are finished, have some students (out of sight of the others) play each instru-

ment one at a time. The rest of the class will try to guess how the sound is made and what material is used to make the instrument.

7. The students can draw a picture (see *Design an Instrument*) of the instrument they made and list what materials were in it. They should also indicate how the sound was made.

Discussion
1. Did your instrument sound like you thought it would?
2. What real instrument does your instrument look and sound like?
3. Can you think of any other materials that you can use to make an instrument?
4. How can you make a "better" instrument?

Extensions
1. Students could measure and record dimensions of their instruments.
2. Have the students make up their own music to play on their instruments.
3. Bring several actual instruments into the classroom. Let the students feel the various instruments as they make sounds. Use a magnifying lens, if necessary, to observe the vibrating of the strings.
4. Create an orchestra. Have all the strings (plucking), percussion (striking), and woodwinds (blowing) sit together. Conduct your orchestra by pointing to the section when you want them to sound a note.
5. Read the poem *Orchestra* by Shel Silverstein found in his book *Where the Sidewalk Ends*. Have volunteers act it out.

How to Construct Musical Instruments

Plucking Instruments

1. Bass Fiddle

Use a two or three pound empty metal coffee can. Turn the can over and punch a hole in the bottom of the can. Thread a heavy string through the hole and make a knot or tie a paper clip on the end so the string won't pull through the hole. Tie the other end of the string around a piece of wood or stick so the string can be pulled taut. Pluck the string to get a bass fiddle sound.

2. Rubber Band

Hold a rubber band tightly in your teeth and pluck the band. The sound will change as the rubber band is pulled tight or loosened. CAUTION — Don't let the rubber band hit you in the face.

3. Shoe Box Guitar

Cut a hole in the lid of a shoe box. Stretch different width rubber bands around the box. Narrow, tight bands will have a high sound; wide, loose bands have a low sound. Pluck the rubber bands to have a guitar sound.

Striking Instruments

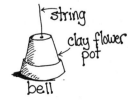

1. Tin Can Drum

Stretch a balloon over the open end of a coffee can or large tin can. Put a rubber band around the top to hold the balloon tightly over the can. Strike the drum head (balloon) with the eraser end of a pencil.

2. Glass Bottle

Glass bottles have different pitches depending on how much water is in the bottle. Get several glass bottles and fill with water to different heights. Strike the bottles with a pencil.

3. Xylophone

Make a xylophone by taping together different lengths of copper tubing or sprinkler pipe. Play the instrument by striking the tubing with a pencil or metal rod.

4. Clay Flower Pot

Clay flower pots have a nice bell tone when struck. Knot a string and thread it through the drainage hole in the pot. Hold the pot by the string and strike with a pencil.

5. Bongo Drums

Oatmeal boxes can be taped together and used as bongo drums. Strike them with the finger tips. Turn over and strike the closed end of the box.

6. Pie Tin Cymbal

Aluminum pie tins can be used as cymbals. Hold the pie tin with one hand and strike the bottom of the pan with the other hand.

7. Plastic Egg

Put some rice, beans, or macaroni in a plastic egg. Shake the egg or hold in one hand and strike with the other hand.

8. Spoons

Get two metal spoons. Holding them in two hands, strike the spoons together.

Blowing Instruments

1. Straw Flute and Trumpet

Drinking straws have a flute-like sound when blown. Flatten the first 5 cm of the straw. Snip off the corners of the flattened end with scissors. The pitch of the flute will depend on the length of the straw. To make a straw trumpet, prepare the straw the same way but insert the straw into the bottom of the paper cup.

2. Comb Kazoo

Wrap tissue paper around a comb. Hold the kazoo up to your lips and hum gently while pursing your lips and letting them vibrate against the paper.

3. Glass Bottle Horn

Fill a glass bottle with water to whatever level you wish. Blow across the open mouth of the bottle.

Musical Instrument Ideas

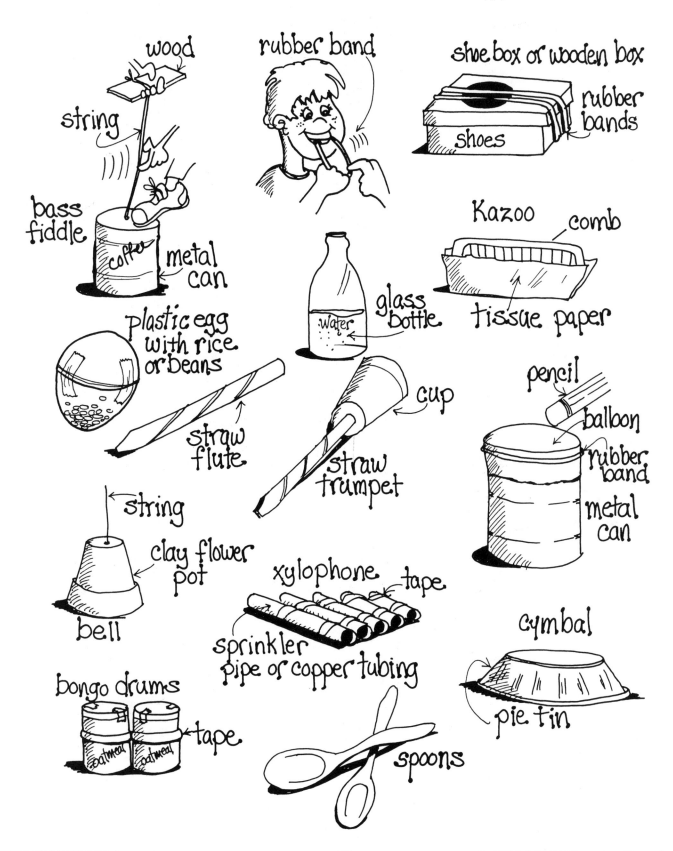

wood

string

rubber band

shoe box or wooden box

rubber bands

shoes

bass fiddle

coffee

metal can

Kazoo

comb

water

glass bottle

tissue paper

plastic egg with rice or beans

straw flute

cup

straw trumpet

pencil

balloon

rubber band

metal can

string

clay flower pot

bell

xylophone

tape

sprinkler pipe or copper tubing

cymbal

pie tin

bongo drums

tape

oatmeal

oatmeal

spoons

Design an Instrument

You are an instrument designer. Invent a new musical instrument that makes sound by striking, plucking, or blowing.

♪ Draw a picture of your musical instrument. Label its parts. ♪

Write directions for making your instrument.

_____

_____

_____

_____

39

Light Energy

Light is a form of energy. Our primary source of light is the sun. Light energy from the sun travels through empty space and strikes the earth. Much of it is changed to heat energy which warms the air. Without this heat, the earth would quickly become too cold for life. The light from the sun is also stored as energy in green plants. Millions of years ago, plants died and were buried by sediment and became coal, natural gas, and oil. Today we burn these fossil fuels for energy.

Light can be produced in various ways. Hot materials glow. The light from fire is due to hot, glowing particles in the flame. The sun and stars are masses of intensely, hot gas. The light of an electric light bulb comes from tiny, hot, glowing wire.

Under normal conditions, light travels in straight lines. For this reason, we cannot see around corners and objects in the path of a light beam cast shadows.

When light strikes an object, it is reflected, absorbed, or it passes through. When light strikes a highly reflective surface such as a mirror, it bounces off in a straight line at the same angle that it hit the mirror.

Objects can be described as transparent, translucent, or opaque. Transparent material allows light to pass through easily. Translucent materials scatter the light as it passes through. Opaque materials block or absorb all light.

Light travels at enormous speeds (186,00 miles per second). When light passes through transparent substances such as glass, air, or water, it slows down. If light enters a transparent material at an angle, it both slows down and changes direction. This sudden change in the direction of a light beam is called refraction.

40

The Eyes

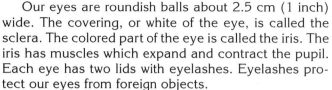

Topic
Human sight

Focus
Students will identify the eye as the organ that sees light.

Guiding Documents
Project 2061 Benchmarks
- *People can often learn about things around them by just observing those things carefully, but sometimes they can learn more by doing something to the things and noting what happens.*
- *Things change in some ways and stay the same in some ways.*

Science
Life science
    human eye

Integrated Processes
Observing
Communicating
Collecting and recording data
Drawing conclusions

Materials
Small mirrors
Crayons
Hand lens

Key Question
How do you see with your eyes?

Background Information
We see most objects because they reflect light to our eyes. We cannot see in the dark because there is no light to reflect off objects.

Light enters our eyes by first passing through the rounded, transparent cornea. The cornea's rounded shape acts like a lens and plays a major role in creating the images we see.

The light enters the interior of the eye through an opening called the pupil. The pupil can adjust to the amount of light by expanding and contracting. It then passes through the lens which focuses the light on the back of the eye–the retina. The optic nerve picks up the messages from the retina and sends them to the brain.

Our eyes are roundish balls about 2.5 cm (1 inch) wide. The covering, or white of the eye, is called the sclera. The colored part of the eye is called the iris. The iris has muscles which expand and contract the pupil. Each eye has two lids with eyelashes. Eyelashes protect our eyes from foreign objects.

After-image is the term one uses to describe what is seen after one stares at an image or picture for a length of time. This occurs after a portion of the retina becomes fatigued by continued fixed stimuli. If one stares at a black image, the after-image will appear white. If the image is colored, the after-image will take on the complementary color. For example, the image of a red apple when "stared at" will produce an after-image of green. Some traditional colors and their complements are listed here:

IMAGE	AFTER-IMAGE
black	white
red	green
blue	orange
yellow	purple
green	red

Management
1. Have the students color the flag before you start the lesson.
2. Caution the students to be careful with the mirrors and not to flash light into someone's eyes.

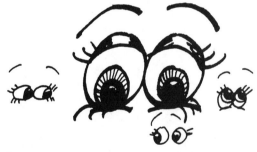

Procedure
1. Give each student a mirror. Ask them to carefully observe their eyes. What colors do you see in your eyes? Have them draw their eyes on the *My Eyes* activity sheet.
2. Have students look into the mirrors again and observe the pupils of their eyes. Instruct them to cover one eye with their hand, hold it there for a few seconds, then pull their hand away very fast. They should be able to see their pupil contract. Have them draw their eyes on a self portrait.
3. Identify the parts of the eye. Have the students label the parts with words on the worksheet *Inside My Eye*. Ask them to circle the parts they can see when they look into the mirror.

4. Give each student a hand lens. Have them hold the lens at arms length. They should notice that everything looks upside down. This is the way your eye actually "sees" things. Your brain turns the picture right side up.

5. Tell the students that they are going to try to fool their eyes! Have students color a flag; the stripes should be alternating black and green, the stars black on an orange field.

6. Direct students to stare at the flag for about one minute, then look at a piece of white paper. Ask them what colors they see. (The after-image of the flag should be red, white, and blue, the complementary colors of black, green, and orange.)

7. Have students color circles or use large sticky dots for the following: Stare at a large red dot, look at white paper (see green). Stare at a large green dot, look at white paper (see red). Stare at a large violet dot, look at white paper (see yellow). Stare at a large blue dot, look at white paper (see orange). In each case, the after-image is the complementary color of the dot's color.

Discussion

1. What happened to the size of your pupil after you held your hand over it and then removed your hand? Why do you think this happened? [the pupil expands to let in more light and contracts so less light enters]

2. How could you test this another way? [go into a dimly lit room and observe the pupil's size, then go into a brightly lit room and observe the pupil's size. Compare the two.]

3. Why do you think your pupil does this?

4. Why does the eye see different colors when you look away after staring at certain colors? [We see an after-image. The after-image has the same shape as the original image but different colors. (This color vision effect is called successive contrast.)]

Extensions

1. Have the students draw and color some other design. Tell them to stare at it and see if they have an after-image.

2. Students have difficulty drawing eyes on an outline of a face. Have them explore features on their faces by comparing the length of their nose to the width of their eyes, length of ears, width of mouth and even the length of their face. Artists use a proportion method to help them draw the features of the face. Eyes are actually close to the middle of the face 1/2 way between the forehead and chin. The nose is 1/2 way between the eyes and the chin, while the mouth is 1/2 way between the nose and the chin. Ears are lined up with the end of the nose and the top of eyebrow.

3. Discuss the proper care of your eyes. Dirt can cause eye infections. Remind the students not to rub their eyes with dirty hands. Looking at bright lights or the sun can permanently damage the eye.

4. Invite the school nurse in to discuss eye care.

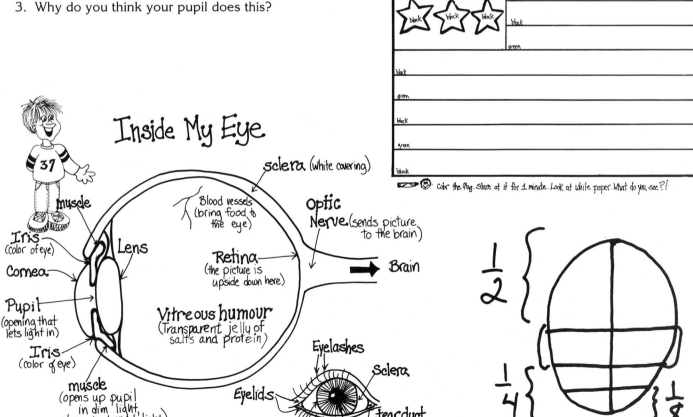

PRIMARILY PHYSICS
42
© 1994 AIMS Education Foundation

My Eyes

Look in a mirror. Draw and color your eyes.
Finish your face and hair. You are special!

Name.

Write 3 sentences about your eyes.

_____

_____

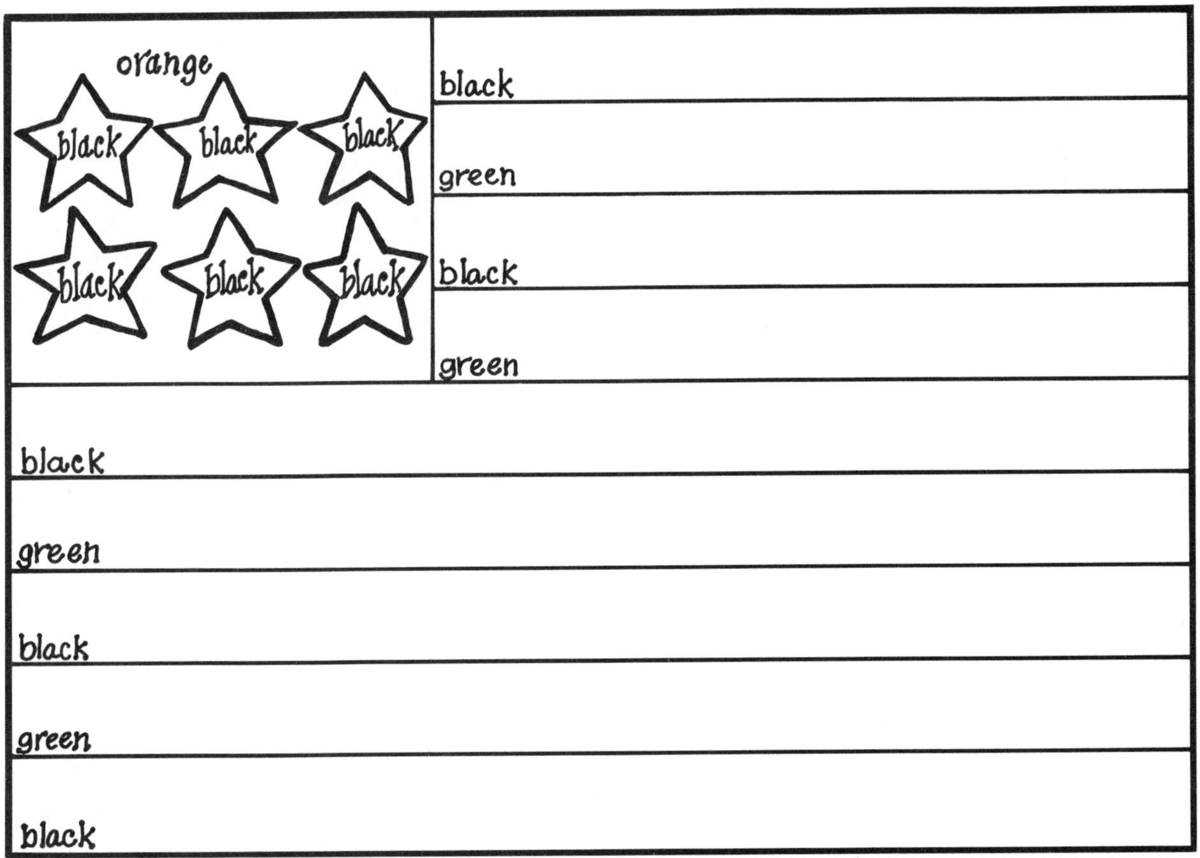

orange

black

black | black | black

black | black | black

black

green

black

green

black

green

black

green

black

color the flag. Stare at it for 1 minute. Look at white paper. What do you see?

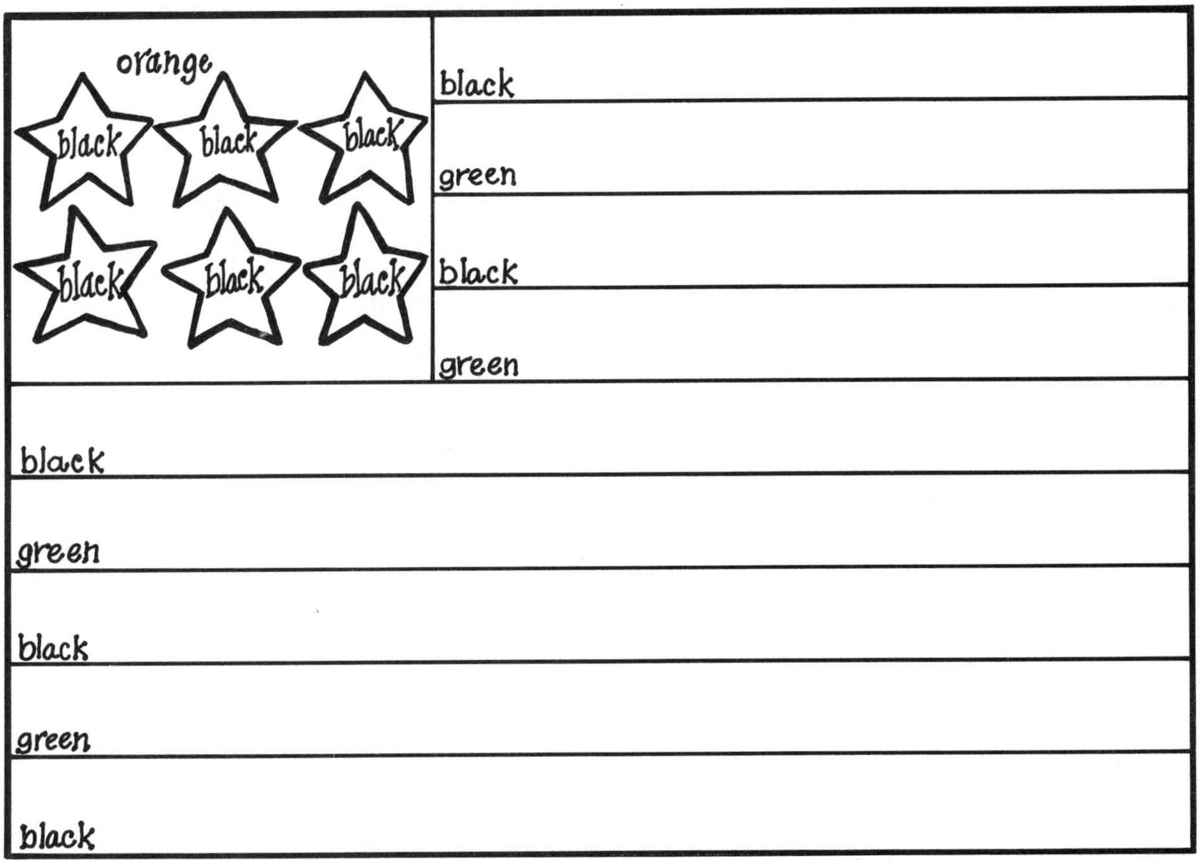

orange

black

black | black | black

black | black | black

black

green

black

green

black

green

black

green

black

color the flag. Stare at it for 1 minute. Look at white paper. What do you see?

Inside My Eye

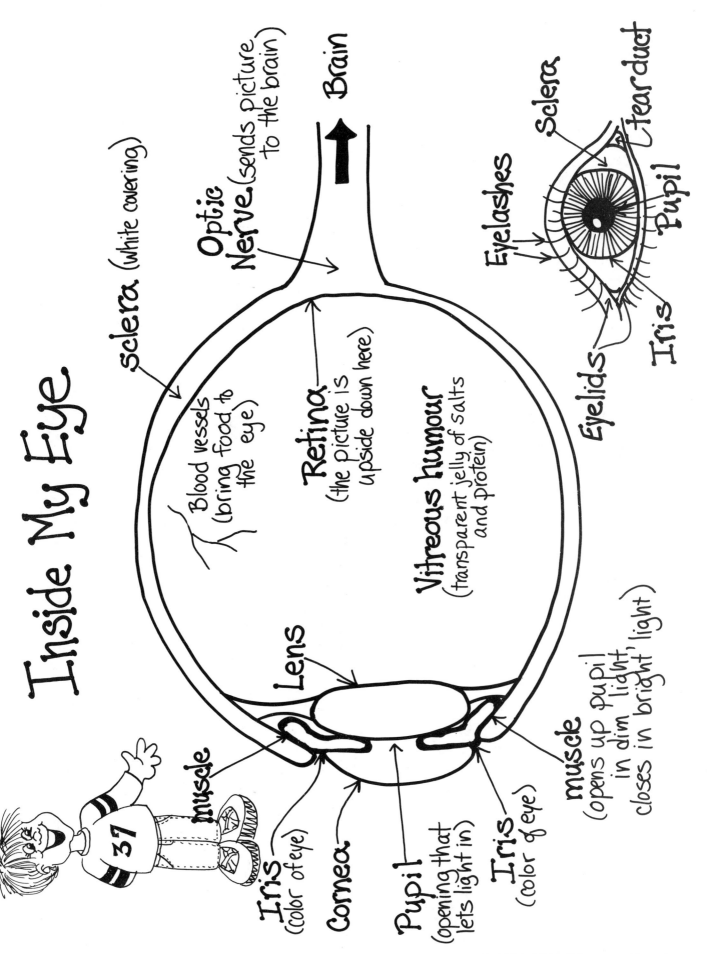

Sclera (white covering)

Optic Nerve (sends picture to the brain)

Brain

Blood vessels (bring food to the eye)

Retina (the picture is upside down here)

Vitreous humour (transparent jelly of salts and protein)

Lens

muscle

Iris (color of eye)

Cornea

Pupil (opening that lets light in)

Iris (color of eye)

muscle (opens up pupil in dim light, closes in bright light)

Eyelashes

Sclera

tearduct

Pupil

Iris

Eyelids

37

Name

Inside My Eye

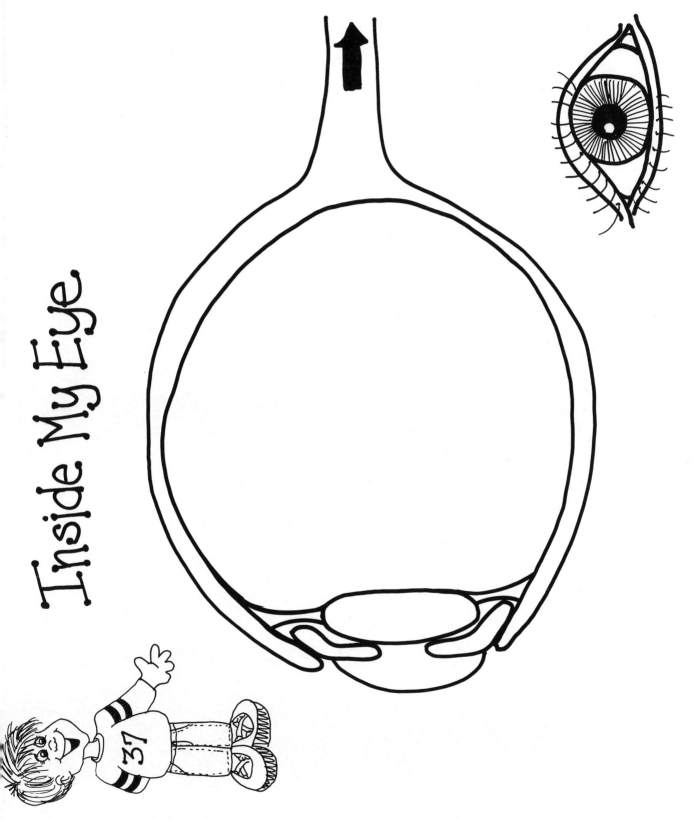

46

Light Sources

Key

Light Sources

Things that produce light — Things that do not produce light

match flame | lightning | water | glasses
lightning bug | fire | plant | pencil
sun | light bulb | scissors | hand lens
candle flame | hot plate | radio | shoe
lantern flame | flashlight | book | mirror

Topic
Light

Key Question
What things produce light?

Focus
The students will investigate many light sources.

Guiding Documents
Project 2061 Benchmarks
- *People can often learn about things around them by just observing those things carefully, but sometimes they can learn more by doing something to the things and noting what happens.*
- *The sun warms the land, air, and water.*

Science
Physical science
    light

Integrated Processes
Observing
Comparing and contrasting
Communicating
Classifying

Materials
Optional:
    hot plate
    matches
    candles
    flashlight
    light bulb
    camping lantern (see *Management*)

light bulb

Background Information
    Light is a form of energy that travels through space. People have learned to make light in order to see when there is no sunlight. Campfires, torches, candles, oil lamps, and electricity have all been used to produce light.

    The sun is the major source of light for the earth. Sunlight heats the earth. Without this heat, the earth would soon become so cold that nothing could live on it.

    Light can be created in various ways. Hot materials glow. The light of fire is due to hot glowing particles in the flame. The light of an electric light bulb comes from a hot glowing wire.

Management
1. Pictures of light sources can be used instead of the real objects to describe light sources.
2. Pictures of lightening, the aurora borealis and lightening bugs can be used for further sources of light.
3. **CAUTION** – All of the items producing light can become very hot!
4. The activity pages of sorting pictures into *light producers* and *not light producers* can be done as a group activity or as a whole class activity using an overhead projector and transparencies.

Procedure
1. Discuss with the students that the primary source of light is the sun. Such other sources of light as wood, electricity, gasoline had their origins in light from the sun.
2. Brainstorm with the students names of sources of light. [fire, electricity, lightening, sun, flashlight, matches]
3. Ask the students why they use light.
4. Have the students look at the page of pictures of light-producing objects. Discuss which ones produce light and which ones do not.
5. Direct them to cut the pictures apart and paste them in the correct column on the activity sheet.

Discussion
1. Which picture shows the major source of light? (sun)
2. How many sources of light are pictured?
3. How many pictures show objects which do not produce light?
4. Think of other light producers. Draw your own pictures.
5. Which light producer(s) would you not want to do without? Explain.

Light Sources - Cut out the pictures and decide which ones produce light and which ones do not. Glue them down on a chart.

mirror	candle flame	sun	plant
book	scissors	shoe	fire
lantern flame	pencil	flashlight	glasses
light bulb	lightning	radio	match flame
hand lens	lightning bug	hot plate	water

48

Light Sources

Name

Things that produce light	Things that do not produce light

49

Mirrors Reflect

Topic
Light reflection

Key Question
How do mirrors show that light travels in a straight line?

Focus
Students will use mirrors to show that light travels in a straight line.

Math
Symmetry
Observing angles

Guided Documents
Project 2061 Benchmarks
- *People can often learn about things around them by just observing those things carefully, but sometimes they can learn more by doing something to the things and noting what happens.*
- *When a science investigation is done the way it was done before, we expect to get a very similar result.*
- *Describing things as accurately as possible is important in science because it enables people to compare their observations with those of others.*
- *Numbers and shapes can be used to tell about things.*

Science
Physical science
    light
    reflection

Integrated Processes
Observing
Predicting
Communicating
Collecting and recording data
Interpreting data
Drawing conclusions

Materials
Per student:
  two mirrors
  Teddy Bear Counter or other small object
  student sheets
  crayons or markers
  magazine pictures

Background Information
Light energy normally travels in straight lines. When light is reflected from shiny, smooth surfaces, it behaves very much like a bouncing ball. A ball will bounce from a wall at the same angle as it is thrown. Light will bounce off a mirror at the same angle that it hits the mirror.

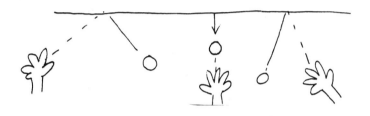

If you hold a mirror directly in front of you, you will see your own image. As you turn it away from you, you will see different parts of the room. What you see in a mirror is not the same as the object itself. The image is actually reversed. That is why letters and numbers look backward in a mirror. The same is true when you look at yourself in a mirror; your left eye is at the right side of your face, etc. A photograph looks "funny" to you because it is your real image, not a mirror image.

Management
1. For *Procedure 3*, tape two mirrors together.
2. Collect colorful magazine pictures – pick some pictures that are symmetrical (can be divided into two similar parts).
3. You can make your own unbreakable mirrors by cutting tagboard or cardboard to the desired size and using spray adhesive to apply aluminum foil or aluminized mylar to the cardboard.

It is possible to make mirrors from aluminum foil or chrome polyester from art supply stores. Fold the foil around a small piece of tagboard then rub smooth.

Procedure

1. Give each student a mirror. Have them hold it up level with their eyes. Ask them what they see. [themselves] Instruct them to move the mirror to the side until they can see the person behind them. Can the person behind see your face? [yes] Can you see your own face now? [no] Give the students time to experiment with things around their desks to discover some properties of bouncing light. Make a large chart to record some of their observations. *Caution:* Remind students never to flash light in someone's eyes.

2. Hand out the student sheet titled *Mirrors Reflect* and a Teddy Bear Counter (or other three-dimensional object). Use crayons to color each line as labeled. Place the teddy bear (or small object) on the small footprints. Have the children place the mirror on the red line behind the bear. They should see the back of the bear. Hand out another mirror, or team up the students to work as partners. Next, place a mirror on each of the green lines; make sure they meet in the center. They should see three images of the bears in the mirrors. Place two mirrors on the blue lines, touching at the center, and they should see no bears in the mirrors. The light travels in straight lines, and the mirrors cannot pick up the bear's image in this position.

3. Use colorful magazine pages or have the children color geometric designs on the *Make A Kaleidoscope* page. Tape together or hold the mirrors like a book to form a right angle. Lay the magazine picture or kaleidoscope page on the table. Hold the taped mirrors on edge of top of the picture. Tip the mirrors back and forth. Move them across the picture for changing effects. Open the mirrors wider or push them closer together and observe what happens.

4. Decode the secret message page by holding a mirror above each word and writing the words below. The message: "Rainbows are red, orange, yellow, green, blue, indigo, and violet. Roy G Biv"

Discussion

1. Why, on the student sheet *Mirrors Reflect,* do you see only one bear in the mirror when the mirrors are on the red line and several bears when the mirrors are on the green line and no bears in the mirrors when they are on the blue line? [Because light normally travels in straight lines and cannot be bent around a corner. On the green line, the mirrors are reflecting light back and forth multiple times, making more images.]

2. When you look in a mirror, when can you see your own face and someone else's face? [When the other person stands directly behind you.]

Extensions

1. Draw or cut out of a magazine halves of objects that can be divided into two similar parts (symmetrical). Samples include: butterflies, faces, and vases. Put a mirror next to half of the picture; the image will double to complete the pictures.

2. Try to write your name in mirror writing so that when you look in the mirror you can read it. (Printing is easier than cursive.)

3. Write a secret message in mirror writing and give to a friend.

Mirrors Reflect

Color the lines. Place an object on the footprints.

1. Put a mirror on the red line.
   What do you see? _____

2. Put a mirror on each green line. Make them touch.
   What do you see? _____

3. Put a mirror on each blue line. Make them touch.
   What do you see? _____

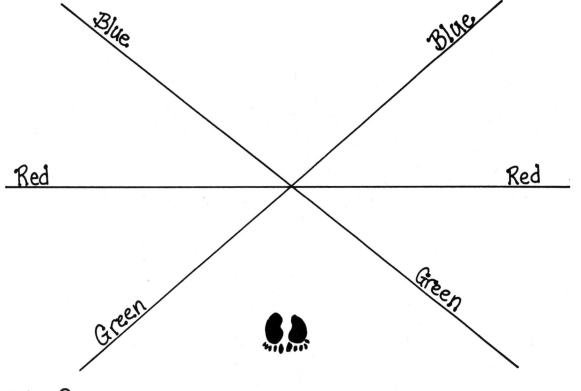

4. Why? _____

_____

Make a Kaleidoscope

Name

1. Color the design.
2. Tape 2 small mirrors together.
3. Move the mirrors across the page.

Use a mirror to read this secret message.

Rainbows are red, orange,

yellow, green, blue,

indigo, and violet.

ROY G BIV

Just Passing Through

Topic
Light energy

Key Question
What happens when light strikes these objects?

Focus
Students will use a flashlight to discover which materials are transparent, translucent, or opaque.

Guiding Documents
Project 2061 Benchmarks
- *People can often learn about things around them by just observing those things carefully, but sometimes they can learn more by doing something to the things and noting what happens.*
- *Raise questions about the world around them and be willing to seek answers to some of them by making careful observations and trying things out.*

Science
Physical science
    light energy

Integrated Processes
Observing
Comparing and contrasting
Classifying
Communicating
Collecting and recording data
Predicting

Materials
Light source (sunshine, overhead projector, flashlight, etc.)
A collection of items to test:
    glass jar or window glass
    sheet of white paper
    piece of plastic (transparency film)
    cardboard
    aluminum foil
    waxed paper
    tissue paper
    glass of water
    mirror
Other items that can be used – cloth, book, hand lens, paper plate

Background Information
Light comes from a variety of sources, but most sources can be traced to the sun's energy. Light normally travels in straight lines. When light strikes an object, the object may allow light to pass through, it may block some of the light, or it may block all of the light. The object also reflects light.

Objects can be classified into three categories. A *transparent* object allows light to pass through. A *translucent* one lets some scattered light pass through but not all and will cast a light shadow. *Opaque* objects block all light and cast a dark shadow. Some objects with a shiny surface do not allow light to pass through but reflect most of it.

Management
1. Gather the objects you wish the students to test (see *Materials*).
2. It may be helpful to have small collections of the suggested materials in bags to be used in group settings.
3. It is wise, too, to use flashlights to focus the light source on the object and to darken the room during testing. This makes it easier for students to decide if an object is blocking light or allowing light to pass through.

Procedure
1. Ask the students to think of all the sources of light that they can. You may want to record their suggestions on a language experience chart shaped like the sun or a giant light bulb. Sources might include lamp, overhead projector, match, candle, flashlight, night light, campfire, moon, glowing coals, television, fluorescent lighting, street lights, and of course, the *sun*. (Nuclear energy does not come from the sun.)
2. Explain that all these sources of light get their energy from the sun. Electricity is made from the burning of energy stored by plants long ago. Even hydroelectric power is available because the water cycle is powered by the sun. The moon is actually reflected sunlight, so it is not a true producer of light.

3. Ask students if they know how light behaves. Discuss how some objects (i.e. windows) let light through very easily. Other objects (i.e. books) block all light. Then there are other objects (i.e. waxed paper) that allow some light to pass through.

4. Distribute the activity sheet *Just Passing Through* and the objects you wish the students to test.

5. (This part of the lesson can be done as a whole class activity, or you can put the students in small groups to test each material with a flashlight.) Show the materials one by one. Have the students predict by a show of hands whether the object will be transparent, translucent, or opaque when a light shines on it. Then test each item by holding it up to a light source. If it casts a dark shadow, it is opaque. If the shadow is light, it is translucent. If there is little or no shadow, the object is transparent. If you lay each object on the overhead, the shadows will be projected onto the screen and easily be seen by all.

Discussion

1. Which objects will allow light to pass through?
2. Which objects block all light? What evidence is there that no light passes through some objects? [a shadow is cast]
3. Which objects do not let light through but also reflected most of the light? [mirror and aluminum foil]

Extensions

1. Hold an opaque object close to the light source and observe the shadow. (large) Move the object away from the light source and observe the shadow. (smaller) Move the source to a different position and observe how the shape of the shadow changes.
2. Use your hands and a flashlight or overhead projector to create shadow pictures on the wall (see *Hands-On Shadows*).

3. Produce a shadow play. Put up a large sheet. The actors perform their play behind the sheet. Put a light source behind the actors so that their shadows will be projected onto the sheet. The audience seated on the other side will see only the shadows.

4. Use a bright light source (overhead projector). Project a shadow of each student on a sheet of paper of white paper and cut out the silhouette. Trace around this silhouette on black paper, and cut out. Glue both images nose to nose for mirror reflection.
5. Make tissue paper stained glass pictures. Post in the windows for beauty.
6. Play a game of shadow tag. Children are tagged by stepping on their shadows.
7. Measure shadows of children at one or two hour intervals. Observe how the length and direction of their shadows.

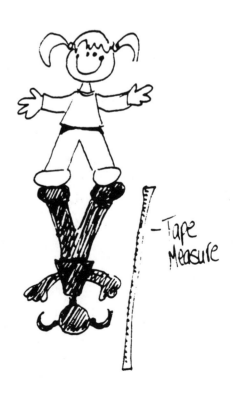

Just Passing Through

What happens when light hits these objects?
Will it make a shadow? Test and mark the box.

Name of object	Lets light through	Blocks some light	Blocks all light
glass			
paper			
plastic			
cardboard			
aluminum foil			
waxed paper			
tissue paper			
water			
mirror			

Animal Shadows

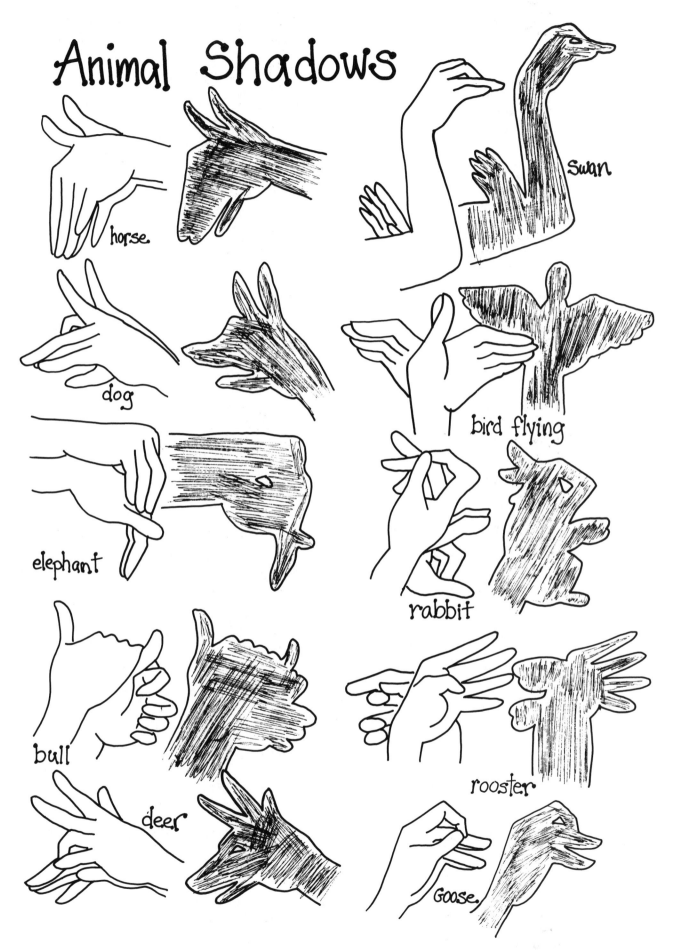

horse.

swan

dog

bird flying

elephant

rabbit

bull

deer

rooster

Goose.

Light Rays Slow Down

Topic
Refraction

Key Question
What happens when light travels from one transparent material to another?

Focus
Students will observe properties of light as it travels through different transparent materials.

Guiding Documents
Project 2061 Benchmarks
- *People can often learn about things around them by just observing those things carefully, but sometimes they can learn more by doing something to the things and noting what happens.*
- *Raise questions about the world around them and be willing to seek answers to some of them by making careful observations and trying things out.*

Science
Physical science
    light

Integrated Processes
Observing
Comparing and contrasting
Communicating
Collecting and recording data
Drawing conclusions

Materials
Clear plastic cup
Pencil
Water
Optional: sticky dot

Background Information
When light passes through some materials such as glass or water, it looks bent. This "bending" of light as it passes from air through water is called refraction. Light travels slower through glass and water than it does through air. To bend, light must strike a surface at an angle. It does **not** bend if it goes straight in.

Management
1. Students should work in pairs. Have one student pour water into the cup while the second student observes what happens to the happy face.
2. Students may use a bright sticky dot to cover the happy face on the activity sheet or they may color it in with a bright color.
3. Students must view the cups at about a 45° angle.

Procedure
1. Give each student or group of students a plastic cup, a bright sticky dot (or have them color in the happy face), and the students sheet.
2. Demonstrate for the students how they need to view the cup at a 45° angle.

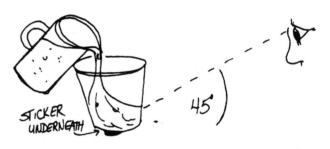

3. Direct them to slowly pour water into the cup until it is 2/3 full and observe the sticky dot. (It will look as if it is rising to the top of the cup.)
4. Have them look straight into the cup from above; the sticker is visible, but from the side – it disappears! The reflected light from the sticker cannot cut corners to come out the sides of the cup. (You may want to place a small piece of tagboard on top of the cup so that the sticker is invisible from all angles.)
5. Next, ask the students to put a pencil inside the cup full of water. Direct them to let the pencil rest against the lip of the cup. Have them observe the pencil from above, below, and beside the cup.
6. Have the students draw what they observe. For fun, let them place their thumb into the water–it will look enlarged and distorted.

Discussion

1. What happens to the sticker (happy face) when you put water in the glass? [it looks like it is rising to the top of the cup]

2. Why can't you see the sticker on the bottom when you look at it from the side of the glass filled with water? [Light normally travels in straight lines and the reflected light from the sticker cannot bend around a corner.]

3. What does a pencil look like in the cup of water? Why? [It looks broken or bent because light slows down when it travels through the glass and water, thus distorting the image.]

4. Have you ever tried to catch a fish in an aquarium and found it difficult? From what you learned in this activity, why do you think it was so difficult?

Extension

Make a list of all the words that rhyme with light: sight, bright, fight, height, kite, might, quite, right, tight, white. Write a poem using some of these words.

Light Rays   Slow Down

Slow Down

1. Place a pencil into a cup of water.
2. Move it around. What happens?

3. Lean the pencil against the side and draw what you see.

Light Rays

Place cup here.

1. Color the happy face. Place the empty cup on top of the face.

2. Slowly pour water into the cup. What happens? _____

3. Fill the cup 2/3 full. Look through the side of the cup. What happens? _____

61

I ♥ Color

Topic
Color

Key Question
What is the favorite color of the class?

Focus
Students will be able to identify colors of the rainbow.

Guiding Documents
Project 2061 Benchmarks
- *Numbers can be used to count things, place them in order, or name them.*
- *Simple graphs can help to tell about observations.*
- *Describe and compare things in terms of number, shape, texture, size, weight, color, and motion.*

Math
Graphing
Estimating
Using whole number operations
Counting

Integrated Processes
Observing
Predicting
Comparing and contrasting
Communicating
Collecting and recording data
Interpreting data

Materials
Per student:
crayons
3" x 3" sticky note

Background Information
Color is important in our world. We are delighted with the colors in flowers, in a sunset, in the leaves of autumn and in the brilliant colors of a rainbow.

Color is important in nature. The colors in flowers attract bees to help in pollination, color in fruit attracts fruit-eating animals, the color in some animals helps them attract mates.

Color also serves as a means of communication. For example, a red traffic light means stop, green for go. On a map, colors indicate certain things such as: blue indicates a body of water, black a highway or road.

A red object is red because it produces, reflects, or transmits only red light. White objects produce or reflect all colors; black objects absorb all colors.

A rainbow is a spectrum formed as white sunlight is refracted by tiny drops of water falling through the air. Each color has a different wavelength. Violet has the shortest wavelength; red has the longest wavelength. They are at opposite ends of the spectrum.

Management
Make a large class graph on butcher paper.

Procedure
1. Use the student sheets, *I ♥ Color*. Discuss what colors the children are wearing that day. How many of them have on the colors of the rainbow?
2. Explain that they will be doing a study of favorite colors.
3. Do the first student sheet, *I ♥ Color*. Children should write in the colors of the rainbow. They should decide which **one** is their favorite color and write that color on their sheets and on their sticky note. Ask them not to share their choices with others in the classroom.
4. Have them predict which color they think most of the students in the class will pick as their favorite and record that on their sheet.
5. Let each child come up and put his/her sticky note on the graph. Tension towards the end of the data collection may be unbearable, so teach the class how to cheer silently or to use the two finger clap to express their joy.
6. After the graph is complete, count for each color and have the class record the results on their own papers.
7. To display their data, have the children color in their *I ♥ Color* graphs to match the class graph.

Discussion
1. What was the favorite color of the class? How do you know?
2. Why do you think that color was the favorite?
3. Which was the least favorite? How do you know?
4. How many more students liked _____ than _____? Explain how you know this.
5. Were there any tie votes?

Extension
Make a puffy cloud of cotton or tissue paper and hang tissue or crepe paper from it in the rainbow colors.

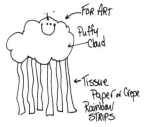

My Name: _____

I ♥ color

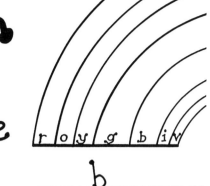

1. The colors in a rainbow are

r_____ , o_____ , y_____ , g_____ , b_____ ,

i_____ , v_____ .

2. My favorite color is ⬡_____ .

3. I think my class will pick the
   color_____ as their favorite.

4. This is the way my class voted:

red _____
orange _____
yellow _____
green _____
blue _____
indigo _____
violet _____

5. The favorite color of
   my class was_____ .

6. Draw something that makes
   you think of your favorite
   color.

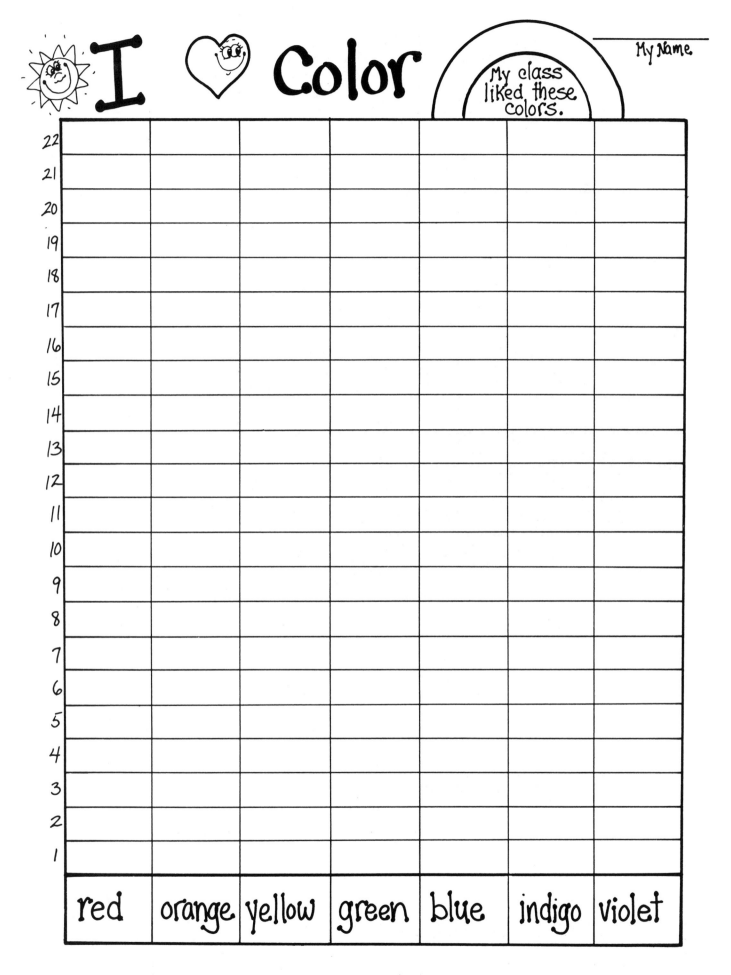

I ♥ Color

My Name

My class liked these colors.

	red	orange	yellow	green	blue	indigo	violet
22							
21							
20							
19							
18							
17							
16							
15							
14							
13							
12							
11							
10							
9							
8							
7							
6							
5							
4							
3							
2							
1							

Magnify

Topic
Light

Key Question
What does a magnifying lens do?

Focus
The students will experience using a magnifying lens.

Guiding Documents
Project 2061 Benchmarks
- *Tools such as thermometers, magnifiers, rulers, or balances often give more information about things than can be obtained by just observing things without their help.*
- *Draw pictures that correctly portray at least some features of the thing being described.*

Science
Physical science
    light
    convex lens

Integrated Processes
Observing
Comparing and contrasting
Communicating

Materials
Magnifying lens
Magazine pictures
Leaf
Penny
Pencil

Background Information
Every day when we look at something, we see through lenses that are a part of our eyes. To see clearly, we may need to wear eyeglasses, which have lenses. The magnifying glass is a familiar device employing a lens.

A lens is a transparent object, usually made of glass or plastic, with one or two curved surfaces. A lens bends the light going through it. It changes the direction that light moves in; this is called refraction.

A magnifying lens is a lens which makes small objects appear larger. Both sides of the lens are usually curved to form a double convex lens.

Management
CAUTION: Never let the students look through the lenses at the sun.

Procedure
1. Discuss with the students why magnifying lenses are used. [to make small objects appear larger] Ask them who would use these lenses. [coin collectors, biologists, mineralogists, students, etc.]
2. Let the students experiment with the lens to see if there is anything around them that they can see better when they use a magnifying lens.
3. Encourage them to hold the lens at arm's length and look through it at an object. Gradually bring the lens closer to them until the object is in focus. Ask them what they see. [objects should be upside down]
4. Have the students look at their thumb with the magnifying lens and draw a picture of it as it appears through the magnifying lens.
5. Tell the students to look at a penny with the magnifying lens. Draw the head side of the coin on their activity sheet.
6. Look at a leaf and observe the veins in the leaf through the lens. Draw the leaf.
7. Suggest that they look at their pencil points, cloth fibers, hair, crayon, fingernails, etc. (Why do we wash before eating?)

Discussion
1. Describe what you saw when you looked at your thumb through the magnifying lens...the penny.
2. What unusual things did you observe when you looked at the leaf?
3. Tell me some things for which you would use a magnifying lens.

Extensions
1. Try to find lenses of different power magnification.
2. What could you do if you were very small or very big?
3. Make a magnifying lens by putting a drop of water on a piece of wax paper. Put the wax paper with the drop of water over some printing. What happens? (It should make the printing look bigger.) Try a drop of glycerin, it works a little better.

Curriculum Correlation
For a Language Arts activity, have the children pick something small from around their desk. Ask them to observe their object carefully with a hand lens. As they observe, they should write down words that describe their object. When they are through creating their lists, have them pair up with a student across the room. Students then take turns reading their descriptive words to their partners and have their partners guess the "secret" objects.

Magnify

Observe these objects with a magnifying lens. Hold the lens above the object. Slowly bring the lens toward you until the object is in focus.

Draw what you see.

thumb   penny   leaf

Pick a small object. Use your lens to observe it. Write words to describe your object.

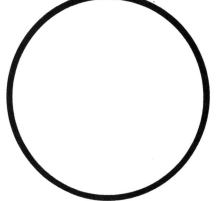

Read your list to a partner and have them guess what your mystery object is.

Mystery Object

Prism Power

Topic
Colors of the rainbow

Key Question
What happens when we shine a light through a prism?

Focus
Students will be able to recognize that white light is made up of the colors red, orange, yellow, green, blue, and violet.

Guiding Documents
Project 2061 Benchmarks
- *People can often learn about things around them by just observing those things carefully, but sometimes they can learn more by doing something to the things and noting what happens.*
- *Tools are used to do things better or more easily and to do some things that could not otherwise be done at all. In technology, tools are used to observe, measure, and make things.*
- *Describe and compare things in terms of number, shape, texture, size, weight, color, and motion.*

Science
Physical science
  light
  refraction

Integrated Processes
Observing
Communicating
Comparing and contrasting
Predicting
Drawing conclusions

Materials
Prism
Crayons or watercolors
Glass pie pan
Overhead projector
Colored cellophane (red, green, blue, yellow)
Tagboard

Background Information
Sir Isaac Newton did many experiments with light around the year 1700. He was the first to discover that white light is a combination of all the colors of the rainbow and every shade in between. He concluded that objects had their color because they reflect that color better than others.

Newton sat in a dark room where a ray of sunshine came in through a small hole in a curtain. He then put a small wedge of glass into the path of the light beam. The light was white as it entered the glass. Newton then put a screen with a hole in it behind the wedge so that he could move the screen and allow only one color at a time to pass through. He observed colored objects in the separate beams of colors.

Newton concluded that an apple looks red to us because it reflects red light better than other colors; the other colors are absorbed by a red apple. A green leaf reflects green more strongly than the other colors, so we only notice the green. White is the mixture of all colors and black is the sensation we get when no light is reflected.

All the colors in white light travel at the same speed in empty space, but have different amounts of energy. When a light beam strikes glass of water at an angle, it suddenly changes directions. This is called refraction. Each color has a different wavelength and is bent so that the colors separate. Violet has the most energy and the shortest wavelength, while red has the least energy and the longest wavelength. They are at opposite ends of the spectrum.

Management
Prior to the activity, make the goggles and color paddles with several different colors of cellophane.

Procedure
1. Show the students a prism. Have them discuss its attributes. Ask the *Key Question*. Record students' predictions.
2. Give the students the sheet called *Prism Power*. Darken the room and turn on your light source. What is the color of the light? [white] Explain that they will look at white light through a piece of glass (or Lucite) called a prism. Have them predict what they think will happen to the light. Discuss their ideas.
3. Distribute the prisms and have the students look through them and identify the colors of the spectrum. Have the students record the names of the colors on the activity page. Then color (or paint with watercolors) the sheet to match.
4. Place a transparent plastic cup or glass on the overhead projector. Tell the class that you are going to

pour water into the glass. Discuss what they think they will see.

5. Pour the water in slowly for a dramatic effect. Hopefully, a circular "rainbow" will appear on the ceiling. Explain that water can also break light into the rainbow colors.

6. Use an eyedropper (or your finger) to drip a few drops of water directly onto the glass of the overhead. You should be able to see small rainbows around each tiny drop.

7. Have the students wear the cellophane goggles or look through the color paddles. What colors seem to be missing? Are the same colors missing with each different color of cellophane?

8. Look through a prism with the colored goggles on. Does the color spectrum look different?

Discussion
1. Name the colors you see in a rainbow.
2. Which color is bent the most?...the least? [violet, red]
3. What differences do you see in the colors when looking at sunlight and at electric or fluorescent lights with a prism?
4. How can you make a rainbow when sunlight shines through water?
5. What would happen if we put water in a square or rectangular container instead of the rounded container? Would we get a "rainbow?" What would it look like? Devise a way to test your prediction.

Extensions
1. Try making a "rainbow" by putting a mirror in a glass of water and reflecting sunlight off the mirror through the water.
2. Make a "rainbow" by spraying water in the sunlight. Each drop of water acts as a mirror and prism.
3. Discuss what makes a "rainbow" in nature. Why are there at times a double rainbow?

Name _____

Prism Power

Color to match what you observe.

White light is made of colors mixed together. A prism shows us the colors in light.

69

Goggles

cut out and add colored cellophane.

cut out and add colored cellophane.

Cut the goggle pattern from tag board.

Have students wear goggles of colors and look at colored objets.

Color Paddle.

Cut 6 of the frames from tagboard. Then cut circles of colored cellophane slightly larger than this circle (red, blue, green). Sandwich a cellophane circle between 2 frames and staple. Add a popcicle stick or tongue depressor to the handle for stability. Observe colored paper, each other, and the world through the paddles. Overlap to make new colors.

Heat Energy

Heat is the name given to the flow of energy from hotter to cooler objects. Temperature is a measure of the hotness or coolness of a substance. Temperature is directly related to the average energy of movement of the molecules of matter as they move about randomly, colliding with each other. Usually, as matter is heated the molecules move about more rapidly and the temperature rises. Usually, also, the increased motion causes the substance to expand. One notable exception is heating ice to melt it: energy is added, the temperature does not change, and the water is denser than the ice.

When matter cools (loses its heat energy), molecules normally move about slower and can be packed closer together. Cooled substances usually shrink and become smaller.

Anything that gives off heat is a source of heat. The heat we use on earth comes from several sources.

1. The sun is our most important source of heat. The light energy from the sun strikes matter on earth. This energy causes molecules to move about more rapidly increasing the temperature.
2. Fire is one of the most useful and easily controlled sources of heat. Wood, natural gas, and oil when burning combine with oxygen in the air and produce heat.
3. Friction produces heat when one object rubs against another. Friction is often an unwanted source of heat for it may damage objects.
4. Nuclear energy can produce great quantities of heat. In a reactor, heat can be produced from nuclear energy slowly enough to boil water and generate electricity.
5. The earth contains heat deep inside. People have begun to make use of the earth's heat through geysers to generate electricity.

Heat energy is used by all living things. Plants and animals use energy from the sun. Humans use fuels to cook foods, provide light, power machines, run automobiles, dry clothes, and provide comfort.

Heat energy is transferred by three methods: radiation, where heat energy is traveling by invisible waves from the source; convection, where fluids such as air or water are heated, expand, and rise, displacing and mixing with cooler portions; conduction, where the heat energy travels through solids such as metals.

Heat Energy & Temperature

Heat and temperature are related but are not the same thing. Most people are familiar with the idea of temperature. The temperature of our bodies is important to health, recipes tell us the temperature of the air in the oven for baking, the weather report gives us the temperature of today's weather. Our experience tells us that the warmer something feels, the higher the temperature is likely to be.

A thermometer is an instrument whose size, shape, or some feature changes when its temperature changes so that it can be used to measure temperature. The most common thermometers are those that have an expanding column of mercury or colored alcohol. A thermostat has a bi-metal strip that curls and uncurls to measure temperature.

Heat energy flows from warmer to cooler. If two objects are put into contact, and we wait until all changes stop, the objects will be at the same temperature. If we put the end of a thermometer in our mouths, heat energy will flow from our mouths to the thermometer and it will come to the same temperature as our bodies If a thermometer is left in a room, it will come to the same temperature as the air. No matter where we put the thermometer, in ice water or boiling soup, the energy will flow in or out and make the thermometer the same temperature as the substance it touches.

There are different ways to put numbers on a thermometer. The scale that most scientists use is called Celsius; the one we use everyday is Fahrenheit. The thermometer is first put into melting ice where the freezing point is marked 0°Celsius, 32°Fahrenheit. Then it is put into boiling water and marked 100°Celsius, 212°Fahrenheit. By making measured marks in between, the thermometer is scaled.

What is Hot and What is Cold?

Topic
Heat

Key Question
What do the terms hot and cold mean?

Focus
The students will learn what the terms hot and cold mean.

Math
Venn diagram

Guiding Documents
Project 2061 Benchmarks
- *Raise questions about the world around them and be willing to seek answers to some of them by making careful observations and trying things out.*

Science
Physical science
   heat energy

Integrated Processes
Observing
Communicating
Collecting and recording data
Classifying

Materials
Scissors
Activity sheet
Large chart
Glue

Background Information
Heat energy is used by all living things. Plants and animals use heat derived from the sun. Humans use heat for many things – cooking food, providing light, powering machinery, running automobiles, drying clothes, and providing human comfort.

Cold means that molecules are moving slower. Humans use cooler temperatures to make ice cream, preserve foods, cool houses and buildings.

Management
1. Have some items that are hot (a metal object that has been out in the sun) and some that are cold (an ice cube).

2. *CAUTION* the students to be very careful when they touch things that may be very hot or very cold.

Procedure
1. Discuss with the students what is hot and what is cold. Have several objects that feel hot and some that feel cold. Let the students feel them.
2. Ask: Is it cold or hot today? Do you know without a thermometer?
3. Brainstorm different words to describe the temperature of things (hot, cold, freezing, boiling, warm, cool, and icy). Record on a large chart.
4. Ask the students what foods they eat warm [soup, hamburgers], foods they eat cold [soft drinks, ice cream], foods they eat at room temperatures [chips, cookies].
5. Show the students the activity sheet of pictures of things that are hot and things that are cold. Tell them they are going to sort them and put them into the two columns, *Hot* and *Cold*.
6. Have the students cut pictures apart and lay them on the worksheet. Discuss with the students where the pictures should be placed and then glue them.

Discussion
1. Have the students explain why they put each picture where they did on the worksheet.
2. Have you experienced all the things in the pictures so that you know for certain they are hot or cold? [maybe not the volcano or the iceberg] Why did you put it there? [learned from books, television, etc.; know what ice is so apply that to iceberg]

Extension
Use cutout pictures to make a Venn diagram. What things are always hot, what things are always cold, and what things can be either hot or cold?

What is Hot and What is Cold?

Cut out and place on a chart [hot|cold] or (hot)(cold).

volcano	water	soup	ice cube
ice cream	candle flame	snow	snowman
chocolate	refrigerator	fire	milk
sun	ice berg	popsicle	match flame
barbecue	stove	drink	bulb

What is Hot and What is Cold?

Hot

Cold

Heat Energy from Friction

Topic
Friction produces heat

Key Question
What happens when you rapidly rub your hands together?

Focus
Students will realize that rubbing two surfaces together produces heat energy.

Guiding Documents
Project 2061 Benchmarks
- *People can often learn about things around them by just observing those things carefully, but sometimes they can learn more by doing something to the things and noting what happens.*

Science
Physical science
   heat energy
   friction

Integrated Processes
Observing
Comparing and contrasting
Communicating

Materials
None

Background Information
Heat energy can be produced by friction. Two objects when rubbed together cause friction, a speeding up of the molecules and atoms in the objects. Friction is a force that opposes motion. Friction always produces heat. If you rub your hands together, you can feel heat caused by friction.

Materials with rough surfaces usually create more friction than those with smooth surfaces. However, friction can be produced on smoother surfaces.

Procedure
1. Put the word *friction* on the board and discuss with the students that friction occurs when two objects are rubbed together. Heat energy is produced by the friction.
2. Tell the students to put their hands on their faces. Have the students discuss how their hands feel.
3. Now tell the students to press the palms of their hands together. Tell them to rub their hands together fast and hard while they count to 10 and then put their hands on their face again. Ask them how their hands feel now. Why? [They will be warmer because the friction between their hands created heat energy.]
4. Let the students' hands "cool off" and then repeat the experiment. Do they get the same results?
5. Have the students rub their hands over their desk tops.
6. Coats, sweaters, and books are other mediums the students can be encouraged to rub their hands across. Each time they should place their hands on their face.

Discussion
1. What is friction?
2. Are you creating friction when you rub your hands together?
3. How is friction used to stop motion?
4. Does it make a difference in the amount of heat produced if you rub your hands fast?...slow?
5. Why do we need friction? [without friction we could not walk – it would be like walking on ice; a car's or bicycle's brakes use friction to stop]
6. Design your own activity that will show us an example of friction.

Extensions
1. Rubbing two inflated balloons together will create friction and raise the temperature. One balloon will eventually pop. Ask the students why rubbing the balloons together made one pop. [Because the friction between the two balloons made one balloon so hot that part of it weakened and tore.]
2. Try rubbing two sheets of fine sandpaper together. There will be enough heat produced that you will not want to put your hands on them.
3. Friction is often unwanted heat energy. Explain that machines with moving parts encounter friction when parts touch. Oil is added to reduce friction. Have the students repeat the *Heat From Friction* activity with lotion on their hands. How do the results differ?

Topic
Skin's sensitivity to heat

Key Question
Is it possible for the skin to sense heat and cold temperatures reliably?

Focus
Students will observe that the skin is not always a reliable sensor of temperature.

Guiding Documents
Project 2061 Benchmarks
- *People can often learn about things around them by just observing those things carefully, but sometimes they can learn more by doing something to the things and noting what happens.*
- *Change is something that happens to many things.*
- *Describing things as accurately as possible is important in science because it enables people to compare their observations with those of others.*

Math
Measuring
    time
    temperature

Science
Physical science
    heat energy
Life science
    skin sensors

Integrated Processes
Observing
Comparing and contrasting
Communicating
Predicting
Drawing conclusions
Interpreting data

Materials
Hot and cold water
Three bowls
Paper towels

Background Information
The skin is one of the five main sense organs. The skin has five special skin senses; they are touch, pressure, heat, cold, and pain. The sense of touch informs us if things are rough, smooth, hard, or soft, etc. Messages are carried from the skin through nerves to the brain.

The skin senses heat and cold and reacts to it. When it becomes cold, the blood vessels in the skin will become smaller. Thus, less blood is able to enter the blood passages in the skin. More heat energy is kept inside the body.

When the skin becomes warm, tiny passages in the skin get larger. More blood is able to flow. More heat energy from the blood passes from the blood into the air and the body is cooled.

The skin adapts to many sensations.

Management
1. Be sure to have water at three distinct temperatures, cold, warm (room temperature), and hot. *CAUTION:* Don't make the hot water too hot to touch.
2. Discuss the sense of touch with the students.

Procedure
1. Discuss what sense organ is involved in feeling hot or cold temperatures.
2. Ask the students to describe what hot and cold means to them. Encourage them to use descriptive adjectives to explain the differences in temperatures.
3. Ask the students if water can be hot and cold at the same time?
4. Set out the three bowls.
5. Pour cold water into one bowl, hot water into another, and lukewarm water into the third.
6. Have a student put one hand in the hot water and one hand in the cold water. Leave them there for one minute.
7. Put the hand that is in the hot water into the lukewarm water. How does it feel – hot, cold, or lukewarm?
8. Put the hand from the cold water into the lukewarm water. Does the water feel the same as it did with the other hand?

9. Use a thermometer to measure the temperature of the three bowls of water. Compare.
10. Do the temperatures of the bowls of water stay the same during this activity?

Discussion
1. How much did the temperature of the three bowls differ? Did your skin feel the same temperature differences?
2. Do the temperatures of the bowls of water stay the same during this activity?
3. Could the same activity be done with a different medium such as metal? Do you think the results would be the same? [yes] Describe how you could test this.

You will need:

3 bowls
cold water
hot water (not too hot)
warm water

Do This:

1. Pour cold water into one bowl, warm water into another bowl, and hot water into the third bowl.

2. Put one hand in the bowl of cold water. Put the other hand in the bowl of hot water.

3. Take your hands out and place them both in the bowl of warm water.

4. Use a thermometer and take the temperature of the water.

hot_____
cold_____
warm_____

What did you feel when you put both hands in the warm water? _____

_____

What is the Temperature?

Topic
Reading a thermometer

Key Question
What is the temperature?

Focus
The students will learn how to read a thermometer.

Guiding Documents
Project 2061 Benchmarks
- *Tools such as thermometers, magnifiers, rulers, or balances often give more information about things than can be obtained by just observing things without their help.*
- *Tools are used to do things better or more easily and to do some things that could not otherwise be done at all. In technology, tools are used to observe, measure, and make things.*
- *Change is something that happens to many things.*

Math
Measuring
   temperature
   time
Graphing

Science
Physical science
   temperature

Integrated Processes
Observing
Comparing and contrasting
Communicating
Collecting and recording data
Interpreting data

Materials
Thermometers
Crayons
Bulletin board thermometer
Optional: adding machine tape (see *Management 8*)

Background Information
A thermometer is an instrument for measuring temperature. Temperature is a measure of the average, random moving about of the molecules of a substance. (More precisely, the average, random translational kinetic energy of the molecules of a substance.)

The boiling point of water is 212°F (100°C) and the freezing temperature is 32°F (0°C).

The most common kind of thermometer is a thin, closed tube of glass. At the bottom of the tube is a small bulb. This contains a supply of mercury or colored alcohol. Heat from the substance being measured makes the liquid inside the tube expand. The expanding liquid rises inside the tube. As the air cools, the liquid contracts and falls.

Management
1. Prior to the activity, piece together the large thermometer and hang it on the wall or the bulletin board.
2. If you live in an area where the temperatures will get below 0°F, you will need to cut the bulb off the thermometer and slip in the page showing temperatures below 0°F, then add the bulb at the bottom the page.

mount paper on railroad board

3. Choose whether you will use the Celsius or Fahrenheit scale. If both are done at the same time, it is confusing.
4. *Before printing students sheet, mark the degrees in Celsius or Fahrenheit.*
5. It may be easier for students if you cover the scale on the bulletin board thermometer that they are not using.
6. The students should how to hold a thermometer. **CAUTION** the students that the thermometers are glass and can be broken.
7. **CAUTION** – Mercury is toxic. Colored alcohol thermometers are preferred.

8. To give students more experience with reading thermometers, it is suggested that they take outdoor readings at the same time each school day. They can then return to the classroom and measure a piece of adding machine tape that will fit the bulletin board thermometer for that day's temperature. Have students record the date and the temperature on the strip and hang the strip on the wall to build a representational bar graph. Students will be able to compare and contrast daily temperatures.

Procedure

1. Get a thermometer and have the students make observations. Ask them to hold onto the bulb of the thermometer and watch what happens to the liquid level.

2. Have them release the bulb and watch the liquid level.

3. Tell the students that the top of the liquid indicates the temperature.

4. Have the students read the numbers actually appearing on the scale.

5. The teacher should model reading the correct temperature.

6. Give students some ice cubes and have them place the ice cube on the very top of the thermometer. They will notice that in the short period of time the liquid is not affected. Have them place the ice cubes on the bulb of the thermometer and notice how the liquid reacts.

7. Have the students take their thermometers to find and record the temperatures in these three areas:

   a. Inside the room away from all sources of heat for five minutes.

   b. Outside the room in the shade for five minutes.

   c. Your body - hold in your fist for five minutes.

8. The teacher should record the outside temperature on the large bulletin board thermometer to demonstrate the process for the students.

9. Have the students color their worksheets from their findings.

Discussion

1. What does it mean when the liquid in the thermometer rises? How can you make it rise?

2. What does it mean when the liquid in the thermometer falls? How can you make it fall?

3. At what level do you think the liquid in an outdoor thermometer would be during the summer? Why?

4. At what level do you think the liquid in an outdoor thermometer would be during the winter? Why?

5. In the winter do you think the liquid in an outdoor thermometer would read the same as in our indoor thermometers? [No, because we are using the furnace to heat the air inside]

6. How many degrees does each line on the thermometer show?

7. What is the highest temperature reading on the thermometer?

8. What is the lowest temperature reading on the thermometer?

9. Discuss the uses of the thermometer in the home, in the school, and elsewhere in the community.

10. Discuss why it is necessary to use a thermometer to find the temperature and the ways its use affects our daily lives. (Remember the Weather Bureau, farmer, airlines, etc.)

11. Discuss what the liquid in the thermometer is and that when liquid is heated it expands and goes up the tube.

12. Do the class thermometers all register the same temperature? If not, why is there a difference?

Extension

Build a thermometer by following the directions on the *Make a Thermometer* sheet. The key to success in this activity is to make the clay seal air tight. It works best if you bring clay over the top of the bottle.

What is the Temperature?

Inside the room

Outside the room

Inside my fist

108
107
106
105°
104
103
102
101
100°
99
98
97
96
95°
94
93
92
91
90°
89
88
87
86
85°
84
83
82
81
80°
79
78
77
76
75°
74
73
72
71
70°
69
68
67

43
42
41
40°
39
38
37
36
35°
34
33
32
31
30°
29
28
27
26
25°
24
23
22
21
20°

65° 66
64
63
62
61
60°
59
58
57
55° 56
54
53
52
51
50°
49
48
47
46
45°
44
43
42
41
40°
39
38
37
35° 36
34
33
32
31
30°
29
28
27
26
2.5°

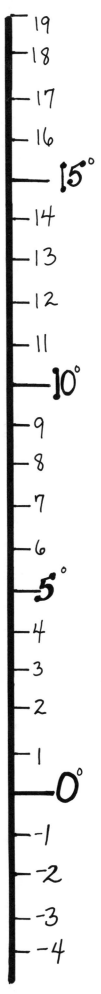

19
18
17
16
15°
14
13
12
11
10°
9
8
7
6
5°
4
3
2
1
0°
-1
-2
-3
-4

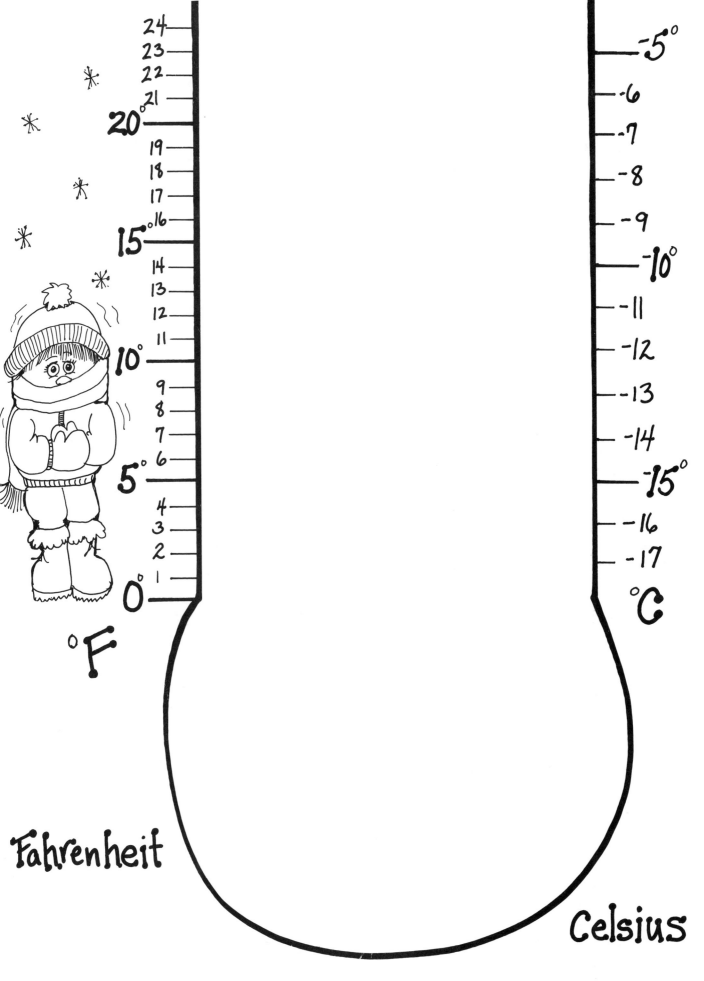

24
23
22
21
20°
19
18
17
16°
15
14
13
12
11
10°
9
8
7
6
5°
4
3
2
1
0°

°F

Fahrenheit

-5°
-6
-7
-8
-9
-10°
-11
-12
-13
-14
-15°
-16
-17

°C

Celsius

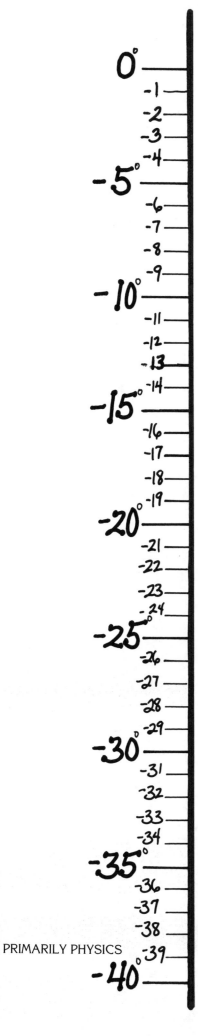

0°
-1
-2
-3
-4
-5°
-6
-7
-8
-9
-10°
-11
-12
-13
-14
-15°
-16
-17
-18
-19
-20°
-21
-22
-23
-24
-25°
-26
-27
-28
-29
-30°
-31
-32
-33
-34
-35°
-36
-37
-38
-39
-40°

-18
-19
-20°
-21
-22
-23
-24
-25°
-26
-27
-28
-29
-30°
-31
-32
-33
-34
-35°
-36
-37
-38
-39
-40°

Make a Thermometer

You will need: straw, glass bottle
clay
food coloring
2 deep pans
◊ hot water
◊ cold water

Do this:

1. Pour cold water into the bottle. Add a few drops of food coloring.

2. Put a straw into the water about halfway.

3. Mold the clay around the top of the bottle. Make a tight seal.

4. Put the bottle into a deep pan.

5. Pour hot tap water into the pan.

6. Watch the water in the straw.

7. Write a sentence about what you see happen.

_____

_____

8. Put the bottle in cold water. What happens?

_____

_____

straw

clay

deep pan

colored cool water

hot water

PRIMARILY PHYSICS   87   © 1994 AIMS Education Foundation

Melt an Ice Cube

Topic
Heat

Key Questions
1. How fast can you melt an ice cube?
2. What is the best insulating material that can be used to keep ice from melting?

Focus
The students will determine ways in which to rapidly melt an ice cube and ways in which to prevent ice from melting.

Math
Measuring
  time
Graphing
Whole number operations

Guiding Documents
Project 2061 Benchmarks
- *People can often learn about things around them by just observing those things carefully, but sometimes they can learn more by doing something to the things and noting what happens.*
- *Everybody can do science and invent things and ideas.*
- *In doing science, it is often helpful to work with a team and to share findings with others. All team members should reach their own conclusions, however, about what the findings mean.*

Science
Physical science
  heat energy
  insulators

Processes
Observing
Predicting
Communicating
Collecting and recording data
Interpreting data
Generalizing

Materials
Ice cubes (same size)
Paper towels
Clock with second hand
Plastic bag or paper plate (see *Procedure*)

Background Information
Pure water forms ice at 32° Fahrenheit (0° Celsius). When ice melts, it absorbs energy. When exposed to temperatures above 32° F (0°C) ice remains at 32°F (0°), but it begins to melt. Heat energy is being used to melt the ice. Once the ice is melted into water, the temperature of the liquid will go up. Heat energy will raise the temperature of the water until it is the same as its surroundings.

Most liquids contract when they freeze, but when water freezes, it expands. Water that freezes in cracks in rocks can split them apart.

Pure water freezes at 0°C, but if anything is dissolved in the water, the freezing point is lowered. Salt is used in ice cream making machines to lower the temperatures of the ice-salt mixture below 32°F (0°C). When salt is mixed with ice, it lowers the freezing point of the ice. When ice melts, it absorbs heat energy from its surroundings, so it lowers the temperature of the ice cream mixture, thus freezing it.

Management
1. Make equal-sized ice cubes the day before.
2. No fire or electrical appliance may be used to melt the cube.
3. Give students a maximum dimension for their keep-a-cube constructions.

Procedure
Melting the ice cube
1. Ask students why they use ice? What would happen if they didn't have ice? Have a class discussion on why ice melts.
2. Have them predict how long it will take for an ice cube to melt if it is left out on the table. Set one out and time it to see how long it takes until it is completely melted.
3. Meanwhile, divide the class into small groups.
4. Tell them the object of the lesson is to see how fast each team can melt an ice cube.

5. Give each **group** one ice cube (of the same size) in a plastic **bag** or on a plate.
6. Tell them that no fire or electrical appliance can be used.
7. Record the time the ice cubes are given to the students. Help them determine how many minutes it took to melt the ice cube completely.
8. Have each group write down what they did to melt their ice cube. Compare the time taken to melt the ice cube of all groups.
9. Have students determine how they could graph their results.

Keeping an ice cube
9. Discuss how to keep ice from melting. [refrigeration, insulated bags, Styrofoam containers] What materials would you use to keep it from melting?
10. Predict how long they can keep their ice cubes.
11. Divide the class into new groups or keep the same groups as above. Ask them to form a plan for making a group ice keeper to bring to school the next day. Limit the dimensions of the device they construct.
12. The next day when students bring in their materials, give them ample time for construction.
13. Give each group an ice cube of the same size.
14. Record the starting time.
15. Have the students quickly wrap the ice cube in their construction.
16. Once every hour, check the ice cubes.
17. Help the students determine how long their ice cube has lasted. Compare the time that each group was able to keep their ice cube.
18. Design a way to display the data.

Discussion
Melting the ice cube
1. What was the shortest time it took to melt the ice cube? How could you tell?
2. What method was used?
3. What generalizations can you make from our results?

Keeping an ice cube
4. How long did your ice remain? How did your results compare with the longest time period?
5. What method kept the ice the longest?
6. What material was used?
7. What was the range of time it took to melt the ice?
8. Why would you want to know this kind of information?

Extensions
1. Use different-sized ice cubes.
2. Make giant "cubes" in plastic zipper-type bags or margarine tubs. Will it melt before school is out?
3. Discuss with the students how ice was obtained and kept before refrigeration. [Lake ice was cut in large blocks during the winter and kept in insulated houses covered with sawdust until used.

4. Make a chart of the number of minutes to melt and number of minutes kept. List every group's numbers. Write the numbers on cards. Put the cards in order, slowest to fastest, or shortest to the longest.
5. Students can make up math problems with the class numbers. (i.e. The red group's ice cube lasted 24 minutes and the blue group's lasted 67 minutes. How much longer did the blue group keep their ice cube?)
6. Break a cube into small pieces and allow it to melt. How much faster did it melt? Why? [more surface area is exposed to the air]

Melt a Cube

My name _____

I think our ice cube will melt in _____ minutes.

Our ice cube melted in _____ minutes.

What did the group do to melt the ice cube?

_____
_____
_____
_____
_____
_____
_____

Keep a Cube

I think our ice cube will last for _____ minutes.

Our ice cube lasted for _____ minutes.

What did the group do to keep the ice cube from melting?

_____

_____

_____

_____

_____

91

Heat Energy and Color

Topic
Absorption of heat energy by different colors

Key Question
Do dark colors absorb the heat energy better than light colors?

Focus
Students will observe that dark colors absorb radiant energy faster than light colors.

Guiding Documents
Project 2061 Benchmarks
- *People can often learn about things around them by just observing those things carefully, but sometimes they can learn more by doing something to the things and noting what happens.*
- *Tools such as thermometers, magnifiers, rulers, or balances often give more information about things than can be obtained by just observing things without their help.*
- *Simple graphs can help to tell about observations.*
- *The sun warms the land, air, and water.*

Math
Measuring
    temperature
    time
Graphing
Problem solving

Science
Physical science
    heat energy

Integrated Processes
Observing
Comparing and contrasting
Communicating
Collecting and recording data
Drawing conclusions
Interpreting data

Materials
Two plastic cups
Black construction paper
White construction paper
Two thermometers
Water

Background Information
Black or dark colors absorb radiant energy with an increase in temperature. Light colors act as reflectors and bounce light off. The black cups will absorb more radiant energy so that the water temperature inside will rise faster than the water temperature inside the white cups.

Management
1. In this activity, one cup should be tightly covered with black construction paper and the other cup covered with white construction paper.
2. Coffee cans can be used with one can covered in black paper and one in white paper.
3. Before copying the student sheet, choose a temperature scale and mark the degrees in Celsius or Fahrenheit.

Procedure
1. Place two pieces of construction paper, one piece black and one white, in the sun. After a short period, let the students feel each piece of paper. Is there a difference in the temperature of the papers? Ask the students why they think the two pieces have different temperatures.
2. Ask the students why it is beneficial to wear light-colored clothes in the summer and darker colors in the winter.
3. Pour equal amounts of tap water into both cups.
4. Put a thermometer in each cup. Read and record the temperature of the water in both cups.
5. Put the cups outside in the sunshine for 30 minutes.
6. Read and record the temperature of the water in each cup again.
7. Leave the cups in the sun for another 30 minutes; again read the temperature and record.

Discussion
1. What is the different in the temperatures of the water in each cup?
2. Ask the students if they can explain what happened. [Dark colors absorb the radiant energy from the sun. Light colors act as reflectors and bounce light off.]

3. What would happen if the cups had been placed outside in the shade?

4. Would the temperature of the water be different if another color had been used on the cup (green for example)? What do you think would happen if the outside of the cup were covered with aluminum foil?

5. What if you covered the tops of the cups with plastic wrap?...a piece of cardboard?

Extension

Cut squares from six to eight different colors of construction paper. Be sure to include one that is black and one that is white. Put the squares of construction paper in the sun. Leave for five minutes, then let the students feel the papers to see if there is a temperature difference. Now place a thermometer under each square of paper and leave for five minutes. Read the thermometer. Is there a difference in the temperature? Which color registered the highest temperature? Which color the lowest temperature?

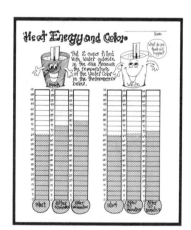

Heat Energy and Color

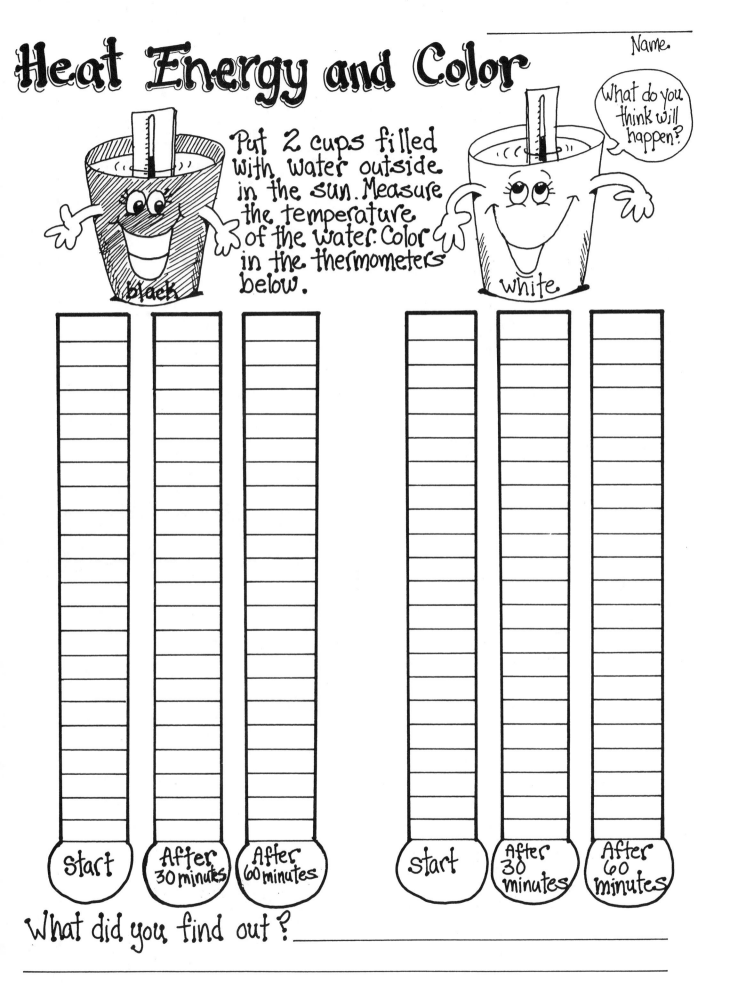

Put 2 cups filled with water outside in the sun. Measure the temperature of the water. Color in the thermometers below.

What do you think will happen?

black

white

start | After 30 minutes | After 60 minutes

start | After 30 minutes | After 60 minutes

What did you find out? _____

_____

94

© 1994 AIMS Education Foundation

When Hot and Cold Meet

Topic
Hot and cold water

Key Question
What happens when a small container of colored hot water and a small container of colored cold water are placed in a large container of room temperature water?

Focus
Students will observe hot water moving by convection.

Guiding Documents
Project 2061 Benchmarks
- *People can often learn about things around them by just observing those things carefully, but sometimes they can learn more by doing something to the things and noting what happens.*
- *Describing things as accurately as possible is important in science because it enables people to compare their observations with those of others.*
- *Raise questions about the world around them and be willing to seek answers to some of them by making careful observations and trying things out.*

Science
Physical science
   heat energy
   convection

Integrated Processes
Observing
Communicating
Predicting
Drawing conclusions

Materials
A large jar or small aquarium
2 baby food jars
Red and blue food coloring
Aluminum foil
2 rubber bands
Hot water
Ice cold water
Room temperature water

Background Information
Heat energy tends to move from warmer objects to cooler objects. In convection, a portion of a fluid becomes hotter (or colder) than the rest of the fluid. Its density becomes different from the rest of the fluid. Hotter fluid is generally less dense than the rest, so it rises; colder fluid is generally more dense, so it sinks. The rising of hot fluid through cooler fluid mixes the different portions, heating the cooler and cooling off the hot fluid. This process can only occur because fluids such as air and water are **poor conductors of heat.**

In this activity, the hot colored water in the small jar is less dense than the surrounding cooler water. The hot water is buoyed up or pushed upward by the cooler, denser water. It rises and resembles smoke pouring from a chimney. The hot colored water tends to rise and then rest along the top or surface of the cooler water. If left long enough and the water is not disturbed, the colored water will then cool and mix with the other water.

The ice cold water is denser than the surrounding water, so the cold water settles to the bottom of the container. Some students may have experienced a temperature difference in a swimming pool or lake. As they dive toward the bottom, the water is cooler than the surface water which is less dense.

Management
1. The teacher may wish to use this as a demonstration and handle the hot water.
2. Use *CAUTION* when handling the hot water.
3. The large container should be filled with room temperature water.
4. The greater the difference in the temperature between the hot and cold water, the more dramatic the activity will be.

Procedure
1. Fill an aquarium or large jar with room temperature water.
2. Fill one small jar with hot water and add three drops of red food coloring. Cover the jar opening with aluminum foil and put a rubber band around the neck.
3. Gently lower it into the large jar or aquarium.
4. Puncture the aluminum foil in the middle and near the edge with a pencil point so the colored hot liquid can flow out. Turn the jar on its side as illustrated.

(Soon the red colored water will be floating at the top of the room temperature water. This is because hot water is less dense than the cold water so it rises to the top. If the colored water doesn't flow out, you may have an air bubble trapped under the foil. Put the tip of your pencil in one of the holes in the foil to release the air bubble.)

5. Have the students observe what is happening and draw the results on the worksheet.

6. Fill the other small bottle with ice water and add three drops of blue food coloring. Cover the bottle with aluminum foil and put a rubber band around the neck.

7. Gently lower the small bottle into the large container and poke two holes with your pencil in the aluminum foil. Tip the bottle on its side.

8. Have the students observe what is happening and draw the results on the students sheet.

9. Have the students write their observations on the bottom of their activity page.

Discussion

1. What did you notice happened to the hot water from the baby food jar? Why do you think this happened? [The hot water is less dense and so rises; the cold water is denser and sinks to the bottom.]
2. What happened to the cold water? Why?
3. What other material rises as it is heated? [air]
4. What would happen if the colored water in the container were left alone for one hour? [If the water is not disturbed, the hot and cold water will mix as their temperatures equalize and the colors will blend.]

Extension

1. Make colored ice cubes by adding food coloring to water, then freezing. As the cube melts, the colored water will stream from the cube to the bottom of the container. Try it!

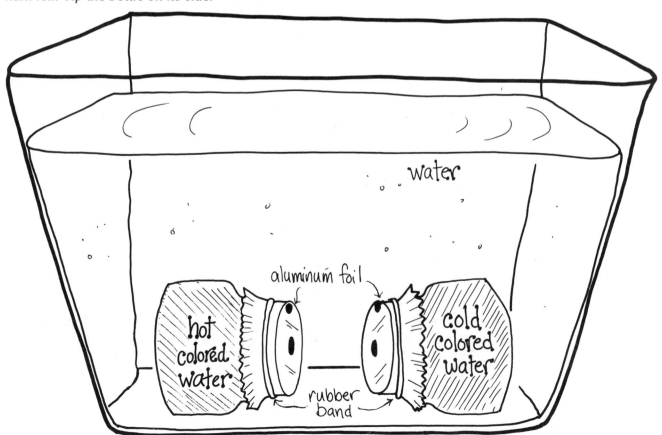

When **HOT** and **COLD** Meet

Name: _____

What do you think will happen?

Draw what you see happen.

1. Put the bottle of hot colored water into the tank of water. Use a pencil to make a hole in the aluminum foil.

2. Put the bottle of ice colored water into the tank of water. Use a pencil to make a hole in the aluminum foil.

water

aluminum foil

hot colored water

cold colored water

rubber band

3. Write about what you saw happen. _____

_____

4. Why do you think this happened? _____

_____

Heat Energy Moves

Topic
Conduction

Key Question
Which spoon will get hot the fastest?

Focus
The students will learn that metals are a good conductor of heat and plastic and wood are not.

Guiding Documents
Project 2061 Benchmarks

- *People can often learn about things around them by just observing those things carefully, but sometimes they can learn more by doing something to the things and noting what happens.*
- *Things change in some ways and stay the same in some ways.*
- *When a science investigation is done the way it was done before, we expect to get a very similar result.*
- *Describing things as accurately as possible is important in science because it enables people to compare their observations with those of others.*

Science
Physical science
    heat energy

Integrated Processes
Observing
Communicating
Collecting and recording data
Predicting
Drawing conclusions
Interpreting data

Materials
Hot water
Large bowl
Metal spoon
Plastic spoon
Wooden spoon or stick

Background Information
One way in which heat energy travels is by conduction. This happens when the fast moving molecules of hot water collide with the molecules of the metal spoon and bring them up to their speed. Metals are good conductors of heat energy. Substances that come from living things, like wood, are generally not good conductors and are often used for insulators.

Management
1. Use spoons that are about the same size; this will help to make the results more valid.
2. If you are using a hot plate to get hot water, caution students to stay away from it.

Procedure
1. Ask the students how they think heat energy moves. Accept all answers; record them on the board.
2. Discuss with the students how handles of metal pans get hot when they are in hot liquids. What have manufacturers used to insulate the hot handles?
3. Have the students feel each object (the metal spoon, the plastic spoon, and the wooden spoon). Rank them from the coolest to hottest according to how they feel.
4. Pour hot water into a bowl.
5. Put all three objects into the water. Hold on to the handles of the spoons.
6. Which spoon handle warms up the fastest?
7. Rank the objects again according to how they feel from coolest to hottest. Is the ranking the same as it was before?
8. Introduce the words *conductor* and *insulator*. Explain that conductors allow the heat to flow much faster and easier than insulators.

Discussion
1. Why did the metal spoon warm up the fastest? [metals are good conductors of heat]
2. Why was the ranking of objects probably not the same before they were heated and after? [Insulators feel warmer to the touch because the portion held warms up. Conductors feel cooler because they conduct the warmth away.]
3. Can you think of other materials that do not conduct heat and can be used as an insulator? (Explain that materials that come from living things, like wood, are generally not good conductors and often used for insulators.)
4. What kind of handles do your pots and pans have at home? Why?
5. Have you ever helped stir a hot pot at home and burnt your hand on the spoon? Why did that happen?

Extension
Challenge the students to find other objects that will conduct heat when put into hot water.

Heat Energy Moves

You Will Need:

wooden spoon
plastic spoon
metal spoon
bowl of hot water

Do this:

1. Pour hot water into a bowl.
2. Feel each spoon. They should be at room temperature.
3. Put the three spoons into the water.
4. Hold the handles of the spoons.

Make your guess!

I think that the ____ spoon will warm up the fastest.

5. Which spoon handle warms up the fastest?

6. Why do you think this happens?

99

Heat Energy Travels

Topic
Conduction

Key Question
How does heat energy travel along a metal rod?

Focus
The students will learn that metal can be a good conductor of heat energy.

Guiding Documents
Project 2061 Benchmarks
- *People can often learn about things around them by just observing those things carefully, but sometimes they can learn more by doing something to the things and noting what happens.*
- *People can learn from each other by telling and listening, showing and watching, and imitating what others do.*

Science
Physical science
   heat energy
   conduction

Integrated Processes
Observing
Communicating
Drawing conclusions

Materials
Metal rod (metal knitting needle, clothes hanger, etc.)
Candle wax
Thumbtacks (paper clips or push pins)
Hot pad or mitt

Background Information
Heat energy is transferred from one place to another by conduction, convection, and radiation.

When part of a substance is exposed to a higher temperature, the molecules begin to move faster. As the molecules move and collide with adjacent molecules, gradually all the molecules are speeded up spreading the energy throughout the entire object.

Not all objects conduct heat energy equally well. Wood, plastics, and some natural fibers are all poor conductors and are often used as pot holders and pan handles. These materials that conduct heat energy slowly are insulators.

Management
1. Use a metal rod, metal knitting needle, or clothes hanger.
2. Fasten thumbtacks at intervals along the hanger by dripping candle wax from a burning candle onto the rod and holding the thumbtacks in the wax until the wax hardens.
3. *CAUTION*: The metal rod can get hot so use hot pads to hold the rod.

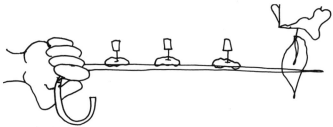

Procedure
1. Discuss with the students how they think heat energy travels in metal.
2. Ask if they have ever picked up a pan that has been on a hot burner and found the handle hot. How had it gotten hot?
3. To show conduction, heat one end of the metal rod that has tacks fastened to it by candle wax in a candle flame.
4. Watch the wax and tacks carefully.
5. How can this be explained?
6. Do the activity sheet *Heat Energy Travels*. Have the students draw what happened and write what they had observed.

Discussion
1. What happened to the thumbtacks?
2. What happened to the wax?
3. Was there a pattern to the way the wax melts and the tacks drop?
4. Which tacks dropped first?
5. What has happened to the metal rod?

Heat Energy Travels

You will need: metal rod (Knitting needle, coat hanger)
candle wax
thumb tacks
candle flame.

Do This:

1. Use a metal rod that has pins attached by candle wax.

2. Hold the end of the rod in the candle flame.
(Ask an adult to do this)

3. Watch closely.

4. Draw what happened.

5. Write about what you observed. _____

_____

_____

_____

Cold Tin and Hot Hands

Topic
Heat

Key Question
What happens when air is heated?

Focus
Students will be able to see that air when heated will expand.

Guiding Documents
Project 2061 Benchmarks
- *People can often learn about things around them by just observing those things carefully, but sometimes they can learn more by doing something to the things and noting what happens.*
- *When a science investigation is done the way it was done before, we expect to get a very similar result.*
- *When trying to build something or to get something to work better, it usually helps to follow directions if there are any or to ask someone who has done it before for suggestions.*

Science
Physical science
    heat energy

Integrated Processes
Observing
Communicating
Collecting and recording data
Drawing conclusions

Materials
Dish washing soap
Small metal can with one end removed
Flat plate

Background Information
Heat energy travels by convection; that is, warm air rises, and this is called convection. Heating causes molecules to move faster. The faster they move, the hotter the air is. As molecules move faster, they are generally moving apart. Because there is more space between the molecules, the air is less dense than the surrounding matter and the hot air floats upward. This is the principle used in hot air balloons. Air is heated by a burner and the expanding air causes the balloon to rise through the denser, cooler air.

When the metal can is dipped in the soap mixture, the soapy water makes a film across the opening. As the children hold the can, their body heat causes the can to heat up. The air inside the can expands and the bubble will "grow" or bulge up over the edge of the can.

Management
1. Small frozen juice cans work well. A can that is too large has too much air for the children's hands to heat.
2. Put the can in a refrigerator or freezer to cool.
3. To repeatedly get good bubbles, let the tin can "cool off" after each use.

Procedure
1. Make a bubble mixture of some water and a small amount of dish detergent.
2. Be sure the small can is cold.
3. Dip the opening of the juice can in the bubble mixture.
4. Turn the can upright; there should be a bubble film covering the opening.
5. Put your hands around the can and hold tightly.
6. Observe what happens. Watch the beautiful colors in the bubble.
7. When the bubble breaks, cool the can and try again. Does the same thing happen again?
8. Record the students' observations on the chalkboard. Have the students write sentences describing their experiences.

Discussion
1. What happens to the soap film covering the opening of the can?
2. What do you think happens to the air inside the can as it warms? [it expands]
3. Do you think you would have the same results with a larger diameter tin can? Explain.
4. Would the same thing happen if the small can was warm when the experiment was started? Design an experiment to test your prediction.

Extensions
1. Pour a small amount of water into a flask. Put a large balloon over the mouth of the flask. Heat the water and watch the air in the balloon expand.
2. Have the students name the colors that they see in the soap bubble and describe how the colors move across the film. Use watercolors to paint bubbly swirly colors on 12" x 18" art paper. After the paintings are dry, they could be folded and used as a folder for papers.

Cold Tin and Hot Hands

1. Use an ice cold can.

2. Dip the top of the tin can in the bubble juice.

3. Hold the tin can with both hands and watch the bubble.

4. Write about what happened.

tin can

GLOSSARY

absorb – to retain wholly, without reflection or transmission what is taken in

auditory nerve – a sensory nerve connected to hair cells in the cochlea, that conveys sound to the brain

aurora borealis – a brilliant display of flashing lights in the northern night sky resulting from electrically charged particles from the sun

buoyancy – the upward force exerted by a fluid on a body immersed in it

cartilage – a tough elastic connective tissue attached to the surface of bones near the joints

Celsius – the temperature scale on which the freezing point of water is 0° and the boiling point is 100°

cochlea – a spiral tube in the inner ear resembling a snail shell and having nerve endings that transmit sound impulses along the auditory nerve

concentric – having the same center

conduction – the transmission of heat energy by the transferring of molecular motion from one particle to another

convex – curved or rounded outward like the outer surface of a ball

cornea – the transparent membrane covering the iris and the pupil of the eyeball

echolocation – the process of finding range and direction of objects by sounds transmitted to and reflected from them

energy – the capacity for doing work or making things move

Fahrenheit – the temperature scale on which the freezing point of water is 32° and the boiling point is 212°

friction – the force resisting relative motion of surfaces that touch

insulate – to keep from losing heat energy or sound by covering, packing, or surrounding with a nonconducting material

iris – the colored part around the pupil of the eye. The iris controls the amount of light entering the eye.

larynx – the upper end of the human windpipe, containing the vocal cords and acting as an organ of voice

magnifying glass – a lens combination of lenses that causes close objects to appear larger

membrane – a thin, soft, pliable sheet of tissue covering some part of the organism

molecule – the smallest particle into which an element or compound can be divided without changing its chemical or physical properties

opaque – blocking the passage of light

optic nerve – a nerve connecting the nerve cells of the retina with the brain

organ – any part of animal or plant that is composed of various tissues organized to perform some particular function. The eyes, stomach, heart, and lungs are organs of the body.

pitch – the characteristic of sound that depends on the frequency of vibrations of the sound waves. High pitched sounds have higher frequencies than low pitched sounds.

rarefaction – a decrease in density and pressure in air due to the passing of a sound wave

reflection – the bouncing back of a ray of light falling upon a surface

refraction – the bending of a ray of light when passing obliquely from one medium into another of different optical density

retina – the back surface of the eyeball that is sensitive to light and receives optical images

sclera – the tough, white outer membrane which covers most of the eyeball

translucent – a material that admits and diffuses light so that objects beyond cannot be clearly perceived

transparent – capable of transmitting light so that objects and images beyond can be clearly seen

vibrate – to move back and forth

vocal cords – the lower of two pairs of bands or folds in the larynx that vibrate when drawn together and when air is passed up from the lungs, thereby producing vocal sounds

The AIMS Program

AIMS is the acronym for "Activities Integrating Mathematics and Science." Such integration enriches learning and makes it meaningful and holistic. AIMS began as a project of Fresno Pacific College to integrate the study of mathematics and science in Grades K-9, but has since expanded to include language arts, social studies, and other disciplines.

AIMS is a continuing program of the non-profit AIMS Education Foundation. It had its inception in a National Science Foundation funded program whose purpose was to explore the effectiveness of integrating mathematics and science. The project directors in cooperation with eighty elementary classroom teachers devoted two years to a thorough field-testing of the results and implications of integration.

The approach met with such positive results that the decision was made to launch a program to create instructional materials incorporating this concept. Despite the fact that thoughtful educators have long recommended an integrative approach, very little appropriate material was available in 1981 when the project began. A series of writing projects have ensued and today the AIMS Education Foundation is committed to continue the creation of new integrated activities on a permanent basis.

The AIMS program is funded through the sale of this developing series of books and proceeds from the Foundation's endowment. All net income from book and poster sales flow into a trust fund administered by the AIMS Education Foundation. Use of these funds is restricted to support of research, development, publication of new materials, and partial scholarships for classroom teachers participating in writing and field testing teams. Writers donate all their rights to the Foundation to support its on-going program. No royalties are paid to the writers.

The rationale for integration lies in the fact that science, mathematics, language arts, social studies, etc., are integrally interwoven in the real world from which it follows that they should be similarly treated in the classroom where we are preparing students to live in that world. Teachers who use the AIMS program give enthusiastic endorsement to the effectiveness of this approach.

Science encompasses the art of questioning, investigating, hypothesizing, discovering and communicating. Mathematics is the language that provides clarity, objectivity, and understanding. The language arts provide us powerful tools of communication. Many of the major contemporary societal issues stem from advancements in science and must be studied in the context of the social sciences. Therefore, it is timely that all of us take seriously a more holistic mode of educating our students. This goal motivates all who are associated with the AIMS Program. We invite you to join us in this effort.

Meaningful integration of knowledge is a major recommendation coming from the nation's professional science and mathematics associations. The American Association for the Advancement of Science in *Science for All Americans* strongly recommends the integration of mathematics, science and technology. The National Council of Teachers of Mathematics places strong emphasis on applications of mathematics such as are found in science investigations. AIMS is fully aligned with these recommendations.

Extensive field testing of AIMS investigations confirms these beneficial results.

1. Mathematics becomes more meaningful, hence more useful, when it is applied to situations that interest students.
2. The extent to which science is studied and understood is increased, with a significant economy of time, when mathematics and science are integrated.
3. There is improved quality of learning and retention, supporting the thesis that learning which is meaningful and relevant is more effective.
4. Motivation and involvement are increased dramatically as students investigate real world situations and participate actively in the process.

We invite you to become part of this classroom teacher movement by using an integrated approach to learning and sharing any suggestions you may have. The AIMS Program welcomes you!

AIMS Education Foundation Programs

A Day With AIMS

Intensive one-day workshops are offered to introduce educators to the philosophy and rationale of AIMS. Participants will discuss the methodology of AIMS and the strategies by which AIMS principles may be incorporated into curriculum. Each participant will take part in a variety of hands-on AIMS investigations to gain an understanding of such aspects as the scientific/mathematical content, classroom management, and connections with other curricular areas. The *A Day With AIMS* workshops may be offered anywhere in the United States. Necessary supplies and take-home materials are usually included in the enrollment fee.

AIMS One-Week Workshops

Throughout the nation, AIMS offers many one-week workshops each year, usually in the summer. Each workshop lasts five days and includes at least 30 hours of AIMS hands-on instruction. Participants are grouped according to the grade level(s) in which they are interested. Instructors are members of the AIMS Instructional Leadership Network. Supplies for the activities and a generous supply of take-home materials are included in the enrollment fee. Sites are selected on the basis of applications submitted by educational organizations. If chosen to host a workshop, the host agency agrees to provide specified facilities and cooperate in the promotion of the workshop. The AIMS Education Foundation supplies workshop materials as well as the travel, housing, and meals for instructors.

AIMS One-Week Fresno Pacific College Workshops

Each summer, Fresno Pacific College offers AIMS one-week workshops on the campus of Fresno Pacific College in Fresno, California. AIMS Program Directors and highly qualified members of the AIMS National Leadership Network serve as instructors.

The Science Festival and the Festival of Mathematics

Each summer, Fresno Pacific College offers a Science Festival and a Festival of Mathematics. These two-week festivals have gained national recognition as inspiring and challenging experiences, giving unique opportunities to experience hands-on mathematics and science in topical and grade level groups. Guest faculty includes some of the nation's most highly regarded mathematics and science educators. Supplies and take-home materials are included in the enrollment fee.

The AIMS Instructional Leadership Program

This is an AIMS staff development program seeking to prepare facilitators for leadership roles in science/math education in their home districts or regions. Upon successful completion of the program, trained facilitators become members of the AIMS Instructional Leadership Network, qualified to conduct AIMS workshops, teach AIMS in-service courses for college credit, and serve as AIMS consultants. Intensive training is provided in mathematics, science, processing skills, workshop management, and other relevant topics.

College Credit and Grants

Those who participate in workshops may often qualify for college credit. If the workshop takes place on the campus of Fresno Pacific College, that institution may grant appropriate credit. If the workshop takes place off-campus, arrangements can sometimes be made for credit to be granted by another college or university. In addition, the applicant's home school district is often willing to grant in-service or professional development credit. Many educators who participate in AIMS workshops are recipients of various types of educational grants, either local or national. Nationally known foundations and funding agencies have long recognized the value of AIMS mathematics and science workshops to educators. The AIMS Education Foundation encourages educators interested in attending or hosting workshops to explore the possibilities suggested above. Although the Foundation strongly supports such interest, it reminds applicants that they have the primary responsibility for fulfilling *current* requirements.

For current information regarding the programs described above, please complete the following:

Information Request

Please send current information on the items checked:

____ *Basic Information Packet* on AIMS materials
____ *Festival of Mathematics*
____ *Science Festival*
____ *AIMS Instructional Leadership Program*

____ *AIMS One-Week Fresno Pacific College Workshops*
____ *AIMS One-Week Workshops*
____ Hosting information for *A Day With AIMS* workshops
____ Hosting information for *A Week With AIMS* workshops

Name _____

Address _____
          Street   City   State   Zip

AIMS Program Publications

GRADES K-4 SERIES

Bats Incredible
Brinca de Alegria Hacia la Primavera con las Matemáticas y Ciencias
Cáete de Gusto Hacia el Otoño con la Matemáticas y Ciencias
Fall Into Math and Science
Glide Into Winter With Math and Science
Hardhatting in a Geo-World
Jawbreakers and Heart Thumpers
Overhead and Underfoot
Patine al Invierno con Matemáticas y Ciencias
Popping With Power
Primariamente Física
Primariamente Plantas
Primarily Physics
Primarily Plants
Sense-able Science
Spring Into Math and Science

GRADES K-6 SERIES

Budding Botanist
Critters
Mostly Magnets
Ositos Nada Más
Primarily Bears
Water Precious Water

GRADES 5-9 SERIES

Down to Earth
Electrical Connections
Finding Your Bearings
Floaters and Sinkers
From Head to Toe
Fun With Foods
Historical Connections in Mathematics, Volume I
Historical Connections in Mathematics, Volume II
Machine Shop
Math + Science, A Solution
Our Wonderful World
Out of This World
Pieces and Patterns, A Patchwork in Math and Science
Piezas y Diseños, un Mosaic de Matemáticas y Ciencias
Soap Films and Bubbles
The Sky's the Limit

FOR FURTHER INFORMATION WRITE TO:

AIMS Education Foundation • P.O. Box 8120 • Fresno, California 93747-8120

We invite you to subscribe to $\mathcal{AIMS}$!

Each issue of $\mathcal{AIMS}$ contains a variety of material useful to educators at all grade levels. Feature articles of lasting value deal with topics such as mathematical or science concepts, curriculum, assessment, the teaching of processing skills, and historical background. Several of the latest AIMS math/science investigations are always included, along with their reproducible activity sheets. As needs direct and space allows, various issues contain news of current developments, such as workshop schedules, activities of the AIMS Instructional Leadership Network, and announcements of upcoming publications.

$\mathcal{AIMS}$ is published monthly, August through May. Subscriptions are on an annual basis only. A subscription entered at any time will begin with the next issue, but will also include the previous issues of that volume. Readers have preferred this arrangement because articles and activities within an annual volume are often interrelated.

Please note that an $\mathcal{AIMS}$ subscription automatically includes duplication rights for one school site for all issues included in the subscription. Many schools build cost-effective library resources with their subscriptions.

YES! I am interested in subscribing to $\mathcal{AIMS}$.

Name _____   Home Phone _____

Address _____   City, State, Zip _____

Please send the following volumes (subject to availability):

_____ Volume I (1986-87) $27.50	_____ Volume VI (1991-92) $27.50
_____ Volume II (1987-88) $27.50	_____ Volume VII (1992-93) $27.50
_____ Volume III (1988-89) $27.50	_____ Volume VIII (1993-94) $27.50
_____ Volume IV (1989-90) $27.50	_____ Volume IX (1994-95) $27.50
_____ Volume V (1990-91) $27.50	

_____ Limited offer: Volumes IX & X (1994-95 & 1996-97) $50.00

(Note: Prices may change without notice. For current prices, call (209) 255-4094.)

Check your method of payment:

☐ Check enclosed in the amount of $ _____

☐ Purchase order attached (Please be sure it includes the P.O. number, the authorizing signature, and the position of the authorizing person.)

☐ Credit Card   (Check One)
   ☐ Visa   ☐ MasterCard   Number _____

Amount $ _____   Expiration Date _____

Signature _____   Today's Date_____

Make checks payable to **AIMS Education Foundation.**
Mail to $\mathcal{AIMS}$ *Magazine*, P.O. Box 8120, Fresno, CA 93747-8120.

AIMS Duplication Rights Program

AIMS has received many requests from school districts for the purchase of unlimited duplication rights to AIMS materials. In response, the AIMS Education Foundation has formulated the program outlined below. There is a built-in flexibility which, we trust, will provide for those who use AIMS materials extensively to purchase such rights for either individual activities or entire books.

It is the goal of the AIMS Education Foundation to make its materials and programs available at reasonable cost. All income from sale of publications and duplication rights is used to support AIMS programs. Hence, strict adherence to regulations governing duplication is essential. Duplication of AIMS materials beyond limits set by copyright laws and those specified below is strictly forbidden.

Limited Duplication Rights

Any purchaser of an AIMS book may make up to *200 copies* of any activity in that book for use at *one school site*. Beyond that, rights must be purchased according to the appropriate category.

Unlimited Duplication Rights for Single Activities

An individual or school may purchase the right to make an unlimited number of copies of a single activity. The royalty is $5.00 per activity per school site.

Examples: 3 activities x 1 site   x $5.00 = $15.00
9 activities x 3 sites   x $5.00 = $135.00

Unlimited Duplication Rights for Whole Books

A school or district may purchase the right to make an unlimited number of copies of a single, *specified* book. The royalty is $20.00 per book per school site. This is in addition to the cost of the book.

Examples: 5 books   x   1 site   x $20.00 = $100.00
12 books   x 10 sites   x $20.00 = $2400.00

Newsletter/Magazine Duplication Rights

Members of the AIMS Education Foundation who receive the *AIMS* Newsletter/Magazine may make an unlimited number of copies of activities for use only at the member's school site. School districts must join separately for each school desiring to duplicate activities.

Workshop Instructors' Duplication Rights

Workshop instructors may distribute to registered workshop participants: a maximum of 100 copies of any article and /or 100 copies of no more than 8 activities, provided these 6 conditions are met:

1. Since all AIMS activities are based upon the *AIMS Model of Mathematics* and the *AIMS Model of Learning*, leaders must include in their presentations an explanation of these two models.
2. Workshop instructors must relate the AIMS activities presented to these basic explanations of the AIMS philosophy of education.
3. The copyright notice must appear on all materials distributed.
4. Instructors must provide information enabling participants to apply for membership in the AIMS Education Foundation or order books from the Foundation.
5. Instructors must inform participants of their limited duplication rights as outlined below.
6. Only student pages may be duplicated.

Written permission must be obtained for duplication beyond the limits listed above. Additional royalty payments may be required.

Workshop Participants' Rights

Those enrolled in workshops in which AIMS student activity sheets are distributed may duplicate a maximum of 35 copies or enough to use the lessons one time with one class, whichever is less. Beyond that, rights must be purchased according to the appropriate category.

Application for Duplication Rights

The purchasing agency or individual must clearly specify the following:
1. Name, address, and telephone number
2. Titles of the books for Unlimited Duplication Rights contracts
3. Titles of activities for Unlimited Duplication Rights contracts
4. Names and addresses of school sites for which duplication rights are being purchased

NOTE: Books to be duplicated must be purchased separately and are not included in the contract for Unlimited Duplication Rights.

The requested duplication rights are automatically authorized when proper payment is received, although a *Certificate of Duplication Rights* will be issued when the application is processed.

Address all correspondence to
Contract Division
AIMS Education Foundation
P.O. Box 8120
Fresno, CA 93747-8120